THE MANAGER
AND THE
WORKING GROUP

THE MANAGER
AND THE
WORKING GROUP

William B. Eddy

PRAEGER SPECIAL STUDIES • PRAEGER SCIENTIFIC

New York • Philadelphia • Eastbourne, UK
Toronto • Hong Kong • Tokyo • Sydney

Library of Congress Cataloging in Publication Data

Eddy, William B., 1933–
    The manager and the working group.

    Bibliography: p.
    Includes index.
    1. Work groups.   2. Small groups.   3. Organizational
behavior.   I. Title.
HD66.E325   1985   658.4'036   84–26283
ISBN 0-03-001438-7 (alk. paper)

Published in 1985 by Praeger Publishers
CBS Educational and Professional Publishing, a Division of CBS Inc.
521 Fifth Avenue, New York, NY 10175 USA

56789 052 987654321

Printed in the United States of America on acid-free paper

INTERNATIONAL OFFICES

Orders from outside the United States should be sent to the appropriate address listed below. Orders from areas not listed below should be placed through CBS International Publishing, 383 Madison Ave., New York, NY 10175 USA

Australia, New Zealand
Holt Saunders, Pty, Ltd., 9 Waltham St., Artarmon, N.S.W. 2064, Sydney, Australia

Canada
Holt, Rinehart & Winston of Canada, 55 Horner Ave., Toronto, Ontario, Canada M8Z 4X6

Europe, the Middle East, & Africa
Holt Saunders, Ltd., 1 St. Anne's Road, Eastbourne, East Sussex, England BN21 3UN

Japan
Holt Saunders, Ltd., Ichibancho Central Building, 22-1 Ichibancho, 3rd Floor, Chiyodaku, Tokyo, Japan

Hong Kong, Southeast Asia
Holt Saunders Asia, Ltd., 10 Fl, Intercontinental Plaza, 94 Granville Road, Tsim Sha Tsui East, Kowloon, Hong Kong

Manuscript submissions should be sent to the Editorial Director, Praeger Publishers, 521 Fifth Avenue, New York, NY 10175 USA

PREFACE

It has been my lot to work with groups in many settings and to try to understand what happens when people attempt to collaborate. In spite of the plethora of research studies, for most leaders functioning effectively in a group depends to a great extent on art, intuition, and luck. I remain convinced that knowledge about group operations can be helpful to managers. This book was written in accordance with that conviction.

In the pages that follow I depart from the usual academic presentation in several ways: I have forsaken a purely descriptive presentation for one that is often prescriptive; that is, I give advice about how to deal with group problems. Second, I have combined research findings, views of experienced group consultants, points raised by my students and clients, and my own views, so that scientific proof does not exist for part of what I say. Third, this book is written to help the manager and managers-in-training—it has a work focus, not a purely academic one.

I am indebted to many gifted people for whatever understanding I may have achieved: my university teachers in organizational and social psychology, the trainers with whom I have worked in the National Training Laboratories, and colleagues in the several institutions where I have held appointments. In spite of the certainty that I will leave out someone, I want to specifically mention Walter Hobson Crockett, John Keltner, Eugene Jacobson, Carl Frost, Oron South, Weldon Moffitt, Bob Golembiewski, Floyd Mann, Bernard Lubin, Ed Jones, Jr., and Dick Heimovics. Deborah Young was of great help in editing the manuscript, with an intervention style that trod gently on the author's sensitivities, and Tita Crabtree ably and cheerfully shepherded the last several drafts through the word processor.

A very special debt of gratitude goes to the students in my Group Behavior course. They labored over earlier versions of this work, giving me much useful feedback. It is to them and to my future students that this book is dedicated.

William B. Eddy
University of Missouri
Kansas City, Missouri

CONTENTS

1

INTRODUCTION

Barbara Boyles sat at her desk and thumbed through the file for the upcoming meeting of the Quality Assurance Committee. How would the meeting go this week? "Better than last week," she hoped. The Committee seemed like a great idea when first proposed by the national office. "Bring the branch's most knowledgeable people together to review deviations in quality and recommend solutions. Focus the best thinking in the organization on the problem." The concept seems to have worked well elsewhere. Why not here? Why all the wandering away from the subject and continued bickering? The Committee had yet to successfully handle an important problem.

What should Barbara do? "Be patient," her boss said, "Wait them out. They'll settle down sooner or later." Will they?

"What could I be doing to get this group moving?" Barbara wondered.

WHY STUDY SMALL GROUPS?

This book is intended to assist those working with groups both to increase their understanding of the dynamics of group behavior and to develop more effective skills for working with groups. It assumes that effectiveness in working with groups is a set of skills that can be learned, along with certain useful attitudes about people, groups, and collaborative processes. The material in these chapters is a distillation of my years of teaching managers about groups—in university classrooms, training institutes, adult education workshops, and in-company team development programs. It is a mixture of research findings, informed opinions of group experts, and my own experience about what is useful for managers and group facilitators to know.

Most managers spend one-fourth or more of their working time in group situations, often wishing they could get away from the meeting and back to work. A substantial part of managerial success depends on getting groups to perform. Yet, few of us have training in group skills. Compared to the hundreds of hours of education in technical or professional specialties, such as budgeting or drafting, many managers have not been given adequate preparation to deal effectively with groups.

I have written this book in the hope that it will help provide managers, and those preparing to become managers, with a usable understanding of groups and how they work. The groups under discussion consist primarily of those found operating in firms and agencies—work units, teams, quality circles, committees, and meetings. These are not, of course, the only types of groups important to the manager. Others include family, church groups, social groups, professional societies, and evening classes. Many of the same principles apply to these groups that apply to work units. However, the focus here will be on groups that are formed for the purpose of achieving specific objectives, while functioning within the context of a larger organization. In these kinds of groups, people usually do not join by chance. They are assigned to membership roles on the basis of the kind of work they do, the position they hold, the expertise they bring with them, or their relevance to a particular problem or issue. They participate on a full-time or part-time basis, contributing their knowledge and energy, sometimes advancing the group toward prescribed goals, sometimes blocking it. Hopefully, but not necessarily, they meet some of their own needs in the process.

There are various definitions of a small group. Such a group, for purposes of this book, may be thought of as a collection of people (varying in size roughly from 4 to 20) who are interdependent—they find it necessary to collaborate to function effectively, think of themselves as belonging to the group, follow a set of rules or guidelines (often unwritten) that define appropriate behaviors for members, and agree, at least in a general way, about the purposes and goals of the group. The emphasis here will be on small groups that rely mainly on face-to-face communication to get things done.

There are a variety of groups in the organizational setting that fit the definition above. One is the operating unit or *work group*, individuals who work for one supervisor and combine their efforts in getting a job done, whether it is digging a ditch, assembling a component for an electronic device, or caring for sick people. Another type is a *management team*, consisting of a middle- or upper-level manager and his/her immediate subordinates, who are themselves also managers or supervisors. This group probably does not work together physically most of the time, but spends a good deal of the time communicating by memo, phone call, and personal visit. They meet at regularly scheduled times, and on an ad hoc basis when needed. Yet another category of organizational groups is *part-time groups* such as committees, boards, and quality circles. Members' primary allegiances are to some other group, but they meet periodically to work on a project or problem to which they have some specific relevance. Still another category is that of the "temporary system" such as *project teams* and *task forces*. These groups may be either part-time or full-time units, but they usually have a predetermined lifespan. They are assembled to accomplish a particular task, complete a project, or submit a report and are then disbanded. Another type is the group whose existence revolves around one particular meeting, conference discussion, or problem-solving session. Participants come together, out of some shared interest or purpose, to learn, to lend their ideas, to influence the outcome, etc. Finally, there is a class of groupings that are "informal" (they do not appear in the organizational chart and are not called together by any official) but which nevertheless affect the organization. These are *informal subgroups* of employees, such as cliques, which may coalesce around lunch-hour companionship, car pools, after-hours activities, and union interests. All the above kinds of groups, while different in obvious ways, behave according to the principles of human interaction. They can be understood, worked with, and hopefully, assisted to improve their performance.

GROUPS IN ORGANIZATION: A BRIEF HISTORICAL BACKGROUND

The original small groups were doubtless families—mother, father, children, grandparents, uncles, aunts, and cousins. Tribes or villages were made up of several family groupings. This fact is important to acknowledge for two reasons: first, these ancient groups had to face many of the same kinds of issues that modern groups face—problems of leadership, resource allocation, rules and norms, competition and conflict; second, for most of us in the twentieth century, the family is still the primary group in which we learn the attitudes and behaviors (useful or not) that we use in functioning in adult groups. In fact, many authorities believe that unless we undertake some reexamination and relearning of our group habits, we risk spending considerable time reenacting in contemporary groups our childhood patterns. If these include authority problems, overly competitive urges, fears of ridicule, jealousies, and other social liabilities, we may well find ourselves less effective and harder to get along with than we would like. Thus, throughout most of the course of history, the human family has been the prototype for the small face-to-face group.

The family group as a unit of production survived from antiquity into the eighteenth century, when in England the family ran its own cottage industry, with all members participating in raising wool or flax, spinning and weaving it into fabric, and marketing the finished product. Of course, in many twentieth century societies some family groups are still units of production, with members involved in such activities as farming or hunting, or perhaps running a motel or service station.[1]

In the history of management there are discussions of the importance of group leadership skills. The Book of Deuteronomy (1:15) recounts how Moses divided the tribes of Israel into groups of thousands, then into hundreds, and finally into tens. Subgroupings were set up to maintain the chain of command and preserve the span of control. The folk wisdom was that any leader needs some unit of organization that is larger than the single individual member, but smaller than the total organization.

The 1920s saw increasing interest in small groups in the field of management.[2,3] As the industrial revolution progressed organizations became larger, more complex, and impersonal, and the experience of organizational members began to revolve more and more around smaller face-to-face units. Thus, even though the formal organization of the work place involved large and impersonal units such as assembly lines, workers quite often constructed their own informal groups. These small groups had significant impact on attitudes and performance. Supervisors who did not understand or rejected the reality of informal organizations ignored an important aspect of their scope of responsibilities.

Mary Parker Follett, whose background included social work, law and philosophy, emphasized the concept of *coordination*. She viewed the organization as a human endeavor, recognized the importance of groups in influencing the motives and behavior of workers, and emphasized the need to educate managers to understand group behavior. Follet is credited with coining the term togetherness. She spent a great deal of time counseling and consulting with governmental and industrial leaders, and her ideas about management contributed to the recognition of the significance of groups. Her writings, including the classic *Dynamic Administration*, have marked her as a pioneer.[4]

The Western Electric Hawthorne Studies are usually credited as the events that first focused major attention on the importance of the internal workings of the small group in industry. Beginning in 1927, Elton Mayo and Fritz Roethlisberger of the Harvard Business School and their collaborators studied and wrote for two decades about human factors in work. They used field research techniques to study groups of workers doing a variety of tasks under different conditions. The studies demonstrated the importance of the face-to-face group to employee morale and performance. Both formal work units and informal groups were found by the researchers to be key components of the organizational structure.

In one study, an observer spent six months collecting data about a group of nine men wiring and soldering electrical connections. The work was routine, and a piece-rate incentive system was used to motivate them to increase performance. It was evident that the wage incentives had little or no affect on productivity. In fact, production was restricted as a result of internal group standards. The most influential control was the threat of losing status in the two informal subgroups that had formed spontaneously. These subgroups provided support, informal systems for sharing work, and ground rules or norms governing their members' interactions. While some of the specific findings and their implications have been questioned by later commentators, there is little question that the Mayo and Hawthorne studies brought into wide acceptance the significance of group processes in industrial organizations and the importance of providing managers with the techniques for dealing with them.[5]

Parallel to the work of Follett and Mayo, the systematic study of small groups was beginning to become more popular within the social sciences. Sociologists interested in studying large collectives such as cultures found they could more manageably focus on groups as their units of study. Early sociologist Charles Cooley developed the concept of the primary group, and a spate of studies began to emerge on an assortment of groups ranging from street gangs to military units. In the late 1930s social psychologists Kurt Lewin and Muzafer Sherif and their followers began to publish studies on attitude change, conformity, leadership, and other group-related topics.

In one of the best-known studies, Koch and French experimented with resistance to change in the Harwood Manufacturing Company, a pajama factory made famous in the movie *The Pajama Game*. Frequent changes in products and engineering methods required revisions in the ways employees did their jobs. Times of change were followed by periods of high turnover, low efficiency, restriction of output, and aggression against management. Monetary allowances did nothing to overcome resistance. The researchers designed a series of experiments in which some work groups were simply informed of the upcoming changes, others were allowed to send representatives to meetings to help plan the changes, and a third variation provided for total participation by all group members in designing the changes. Results dramatically demonstrated that the greater the degree of worker participation in redesigning the work, the faster the recovery of productivity and the lower the rates of turnover and aggression.

By the time Lewin founded the Research Center for Group Dynamics at the Massachusetts Institute of Technology in 1945, the field of small groups research was fully established. Exploration of some of the more practical applications of group processes in organizations could proceed more rapidly because the necessary concepts, terminology, and research methods were now becoming available.[6]

In the late 1940s and 1950s research and applied writing and training began in earnest. Part of the impetus came from contract research projects sponsored by the armed forces out of a need to better understand how to staff and manage small groups such as submarine and airplane crews operating under complex and stressful situations. Another significant thrust came from Lewin's followers, who were interested in understanding democratic leadership methods. Their work led to sensitivity training in interpersonal relationships, utilizing the small group as the basic training unit.[7] Thousands of administrators were introduced to group processes through programs sponsored by the National Training Laboratories, the American Management Association, and other organizations. The new awareness of groups was also carried into other social science fields, including adult education conference methods, group psychotherapy, and self-help efforts such as Alcoholics Anonymous. Scientific journals and management magazines began to publish articles on groups, and for the first time several books were published which pulled together what was known or suspected about the dynamics of groups. By 1962 Golembiewski was able to survey the research literature and begin the process of isolating the major variables and dimensions of group operation.[8]

GROUPS IN MODERN ORGANIZATIONS

A milestone in the application of small group technology in industry occurred in 1961 when Rensis Likert, director of the University of Michigan's Institute for Social Research, published *New Patterns in Management*.[9] The book synthesized over a decade of applied research in a large number of organizations. Findings clearly demonstrated that one of the performance factors that distinguished effective from ineffective managers was that the effective managers dealt with their subordinates as groups or teams rather than on a one-to-one basis. Groups with higher peer group pride, loyalty, and common goals showed higher productivity. Workers in such groups exhibited more cooperation and sharing of work. The cohesive groups with high peer loyalty were also found to have more positive attitudes toward their jobs and the company, and higher production goals. Evidence was cited that illustrated the importance of groups in influencing the overall performance of the organization. Work groups, not individuals, were identified as the basic building blocks of the organization. Effective managers work to improve group functioning.

A series of studies by Trist and others at the Tavistock Institute in Great Britain illustrated how, under certain circumstances, the impact of group factors can go dramatically beyond even loyalty and productivity. Mechanization of the English coal mines necessitated the reorganization of work methods and the breaking up of long-standing small work teams. These teams had not only performed work functions but had helped provide important degrees of safety, support, and comfort under very adverse working conditions. Marked increases in the incidence of physical and emotional illness, absenteeism, and turnover occurred after reorganization. The studies indicated the direct relationships between these human problems and the break-up of the close-knit work teams. Subsequent experiments brought about increased productivity and satisfaction by redesigning the system to include stable and autonomous face-to-face teams.[10]

Other studies began to document ways in which groups could be utilized to enhance productivity. Robert Blake and Jane Mouton[11] and Jay Hall[12] demonstrated that, under certain conditions, groups make better decisions than do individuals. The literature on programs for overcoming resistance to change emphasized the use of group training techniques. And new approaches to employee training utilized group-oriented methods such as conference discussions, case analysis, and role playing. In short, the group had come into its own in the complex organizational setting.

Another set of rationales for the importance of groups was provided by the economist John Kenneth Galbraith, who asserted, "One can do worse than think of a business organization as a hierarchy of committees."[13] According to Galbraith, organizations function as a *group of groups*, because the large number of decisions that need to be made must draw on the knowledge, experience, and intuition of more than one person. The complexity, technological sophistication, and need for planning that characterize modern organizations require the pooling of information from a wide variety of specialists whose expertise often runs deep but narrow. Further, the expertise must not only be pooled, but coordinated. Committees and other similar arrangements enhance communication among the various specialists and organizational segments involved and encourage their commitment and support for plans that they have been involved in formulating. For example, this approach has been found particularly effective in the introduction of new technology, such as word processing systems, into the workplace.

Additional impetus for understanding groups and improving their effectiveness has come about as a result of the development of newer, more flexible forms of organization structure. In many fields the traditional pyramid has been altered or augmented (if not replaced) by matrix organizations, project groups, task forces, quality circles, and other temporary systems. These structures are frequently devised to fulfill specific functions and operate independently on the basis of face-to-face relationships with less dependence on rules and traditions.

Recent industrial experiences have focused the attention of managers on groups as key elements in production. *Autonomous work groups* function without traditional close supervision and hierarchy. The groups make many of their own personnel, fiscal, and operational decisions, rotate among jobs and schedule work flow. *Quality circles*, popularized in writings about Japanese management, are asked to take broader responsibility for product quality, production efficiency, and quality of work life than are workers in traditional organizations. We will discuss these groups in a later chapter in this book. At this point they are mentioned to highlight the fact that as groups are given increasingly important roles in production, the effectiveness of these groups becomes crucial. Such arrangements place heavy emphasis on group effectiveness and require leaders who know how to build teams and facilitate communication, resolve conflicts, and in a variety of other ways provide the cohesion to hold together a group.[14] Organization development techniques, such as team building, are examples of group-oriented training approaches that have been devised to help managers learn to work effectively with teams and groups.

ISSUES IN THE STUDY OF GROUPS

As we investigate groups it is useful to prepare ourselves for the task by considering several issues about groups and their study that may get in the way of better understanding. The following points may help avoid some common pitfalls.

Complexity

Groups are complex. A group is an arena in which the history, goals, fears, styles, and skills of the members are played out through thousands of interactions. Helping a group to improve its functioning is not simple. Methods for improving group performance are available, but they are imperfect. It is rarely useful to order people to cooperate more positively, to communicate more clearly, or to raise their levels of commitment. Rather, they must be helped to learn methods for better cooperation and to identify blockages to cooperation in their group. They must learn to improve group communication by continually testing the accuracy of their messages to each other. And they must work on commitment by dealing with their own personal goals as they coincide with or differ from group or organizational goals.

Some managers are skeptical about the possibility of a practical science of group behavior. "Human behavior is too complex and unpredictable," they say. "We can't even understand one human being and predict what he or she will do. How can we possibly predict what will happen when a dozen of them get together to work on a complicated task?"

It is true that the study of behavior in any setting is an inexact science, and groups are certainly no exception. The large number of interrelated variables present, both within the individuals and within the situation, and the many interactions that take place over time, make exact predictions risky. But it is possible to develop models of group interaction—ways of looking at groups that help identify some of the major variables and put them into categories in order to sort out what is going on.

When we observe a group of people in operation, what we see at the most simple and naturalistic level is a number of human beings congregated in a given place, talking (usually) with each other and (sometimes) moving physical objects around. If this "blooming buzzing confusion" were all we could discern, developing skills in working with groups would indeed be difficult. But suppose we are given categories of behavior to look for, categories that others have found useful in their attempts to understand groups. These "handles" may then allow us to see some things we didn't see before. For example, suppose it is suggested that we keep track of *interaction patterns*, that is, the frequency with which each member talks with each other member. This simple technique, it turns out, allows us to make educated guesses about several aspects of the group, including leadership, involvement, subgroups, and even the degree to which members are listening to and responding to each other.

Even though the accumulation of studies on groups provides much more material than can be included in any single book, current knowledge is far from complete. There are differing theories about group behavior; each one provides its own perspective while overlapping with others. Which theory is "best" is difficult to determine. Theories should be judged on the basis of their utility. Do they allow the user to explain and understand and (hopefully) predict? Further, all that is known about groups is not found in controlled laboratory studies. Experienced managers, group observers, leaders, and trainers have made significant contributions to the state of the art, as have scientists. The current state of development of research and theory about groups provides a challenge to the would-be user to sort out and synthesize those elements that will provide practical utility.

Bias in Observation

When we observe groups, using the models and concepts from this book, or any book, we are imposing *meaning* on the situation. That is, we gather data, analyze it, and interpret it according to a pre-established schema. If the schema is well thought out and validated for groups like the one we are studying, if we are skilled and careful in our observation, and if we can interpret our findings objectively, with a minimum of bias or preconception, we stand a good chance of achieving a "valid" picture of the group, at least in the sense that other objective observers would obtain similar findings. On the other hand, if we use shoddy or oversimplified models of behavior (such as those found in the Sunday newspaper supplement or delivered sugar-coated by after-dinner speakers), if we are not careful to be objective about what we see, or if we let our wishes and biases creep into our interpretations, we can find ourselves with results that are not only invalid, but perhaps detrimental to our efforts to improve the group. Thus, the manager who doesn't want to believe that his group has the potential to make good decisions without him finds it all too easy to say, "See, I told you this group can't make its own decisions." Or the group member who is firmly convinced that she isn't appreciated by the group will have no trouble finding evidence to verify that fact, if she wants to badly enough. My admonition, of course, is to identify, own up to, and guard against our own biases. The group situation can sometimes become a mirror in which we find our own needs, problems, and blind spots. Self-understanding and a willingness to consider viewpoints different from our own are prerequisites to effective group leadership.

Resistance to Groups

Many managers have reservations about working in groups. ("The camel is a horse built by a committee.") For some, deeply held values about individualism and responsibility are paramount, and anything that enmeshes one in a "groupy" setting is distasteful. For others, groups feel uncomfortable. The solitude and relative safety of working alone or with one or two other people is preferred to the necessity of interacting with (and thus making ourselves vulnerable to) a dozen others, with all their biases, self-interests, suspicions, and jealousies. Perhaps still others fear that the group will take advantage of them and use their ideas or skills, making them the property of the group and not giving anything in return. Such reservations are to be respected. This book is not intended to sell managers the value of groups in organizations. Groups are a part of the reality of most organizations, and if they are, it is better to deal with them effectively rather than ineffectively. As suggested earlier, people cluster in small groups for a variety of reasons—because of habit, need for social interaction and support, to work on tasks together, to pool information, and so on. Some groups are highly effective at solving problems; others are ineffective. Some groups enhance the morale and satisfaction of their members; others cause unhappiness, conflict, and alienation. Some groups support freedom and creativity; others stifle their members. Some groups meet too frequently and spend (waste) too much time together; others don't meet often enough to build the teamwork necessary for effective collaboration.

For people who work with groups, perhaps the most important need is to avoid the feeling that the group is out of control, that once it starts on its course nothing can be done to change it. The major premise of this book is that groups can be more effective. If a decision is made that a group is a useful mechanism in a given situation, then it is folly simply to collect the members and start it functioning without attention to those steps necessary to increase the probability of success. And, as the group runs its course, if we see that it is not doing what it is supposed to be doing, it is folly not to intervene to change its process.

ORGANIZATION OF THIS BOOK

One cannot develop practical group skills simply by reading a book (or a hundred books). Taking part in group activities and then evaluating them makes for useful learning. Each chapter, therefore, contains materials that are designed to help you engage in an experiential learning process. If this book is used in courses or workshops, it is suggested that discussion groups be formed for the purpose of practicing the Learning Aids provided at the end of each chapter. If it is used outside the classroom by managers who want to learn to be more effective in the groups they work with, it is suggested that they try out some of the techniques in their groups.

The organization of the book is intended to take the reader through a progression of topics useful in understanding and using group dynamics. Chapter 2 is a review of information about human behavior, material that helps us to understand people as group members, the things that influence their actions and cause them to behave the way they do. Chapter 3 focuses on the impact of cultural factors on members' behavior—the attitudes, values, and preconceptions we bring into the group with us.

Chapter 4 introduces the study of groups. It provides the basic concepts and ways of observing groups that the rest of the book will build on, providing information for application. Chapter 5 is about group leadership. What skills, attitudes, procedures, etc., are helpful to the leader as he/she strives to facilitate a group's movement toward effectiveness? Chapter 6 deals with the most common process issues in groups—those aspects, such as communication and conflict, that most often become trouble spots as a group strives to coordinate the efforts of its members. Chapter 7 focuses specifically on task accomplishment, the factors that bear most directly on decision making, problem solving, productivity, and the like. Chapter 8 deals with the application of group technique in special situations, such as conducting meetings, team building, task force management, and groups for support and learning.

This book contains only a fraction of the published information now available about groups. It is my hope and belief that the concepts selected for inclusion are among the more useful. The book also attempts to tread a path that avoids heavy emphasis on theory and research, on the one hand, and overly simplistic pop psychology, on the other hand. This compromise will probably meet with disapproval from some in both camps. However, it has been my experience that when one is in the middle of a complex and volatile group interaction, it's like riding a surfboard—the key word is balance. Sound and applicable skills and principles are needed, not complicated and abstract theories nor glib and simplistic truisms.

My hope is that after you have read this book and tried out the Learning Aids you will have evolved your own usable approach to understanding and working with groups.

LEARNING AIDS

The following activities are designed to help you apply some of the ideas discussed in this chapter to your own life and work. It is suggested that you think about and respond to the items on your own, and then discuss them with another person or a group.

1. Make a list of the significant small groups that you belong to, including those that you lead. Include groups at work (work units, committees, etc.) and at home (family, roommates, etc.), as well as social and professional groups. Take some time to develop the list because it will be used in Learning Aids sections in later chapters.

   I. _____
   II. _____
   III. _____
   IV. _____
   V. _____
   VI. _____
   VII. _____
   VIII. _____

2. Group relationships may be categorized according to the *purpose(s)* that they are intended to fulfill. Most groups fall into one or more of the following categories.
   A. *Emotional–expressive.* Relationships formed for the purpose of fulfilling ourselves. Examples are love, marriage and family, friendships.
   B. *Learning and comprehending reality.* Relationships for the purpose of gaining more information about one's self or significant aspects of the world. Examples are college courses, study groups, and adult education classes.

C. *Change or influence.* Relationships for the purpose of bringing about some improvement in members or in the group. Self-development groups, therapy or encounter groups, and religious organizations are examples.

D. *Instrumental.* Members cooperate to achieve some task or tangible goal. Performance judged by output and by members' ability to work together. Work groups, task forces, and committees.

Go back over the list you developed in Item 1 and indicate with A, B, C, or D in the left margin which of the above categories each of your groups falls into. Since most groups are not pure types, do not be surprised if a group falls into more than one category.

3. Again refer back to your list of groups in Item 1 and pick one group that you want to better understand and improve.
   A. What is the "official" purpose of the group in terms of the categories in Item 2? That is, was it formed primarily for the purpose of accomplishing a task (work group), providing emotional fulfillment (family), etc.?
   B. Are there other categories from Item 2 that also make up important aspects of the group's existence? Are these understood by the group?
   C. Write down five or six adjectives that describe your feelings when you think about this group (friendly, distant, hectic, etc.).
   D. What problems is the group having?

4. Your time spent reading this book will have been worthwhile if by the end you have identified one or more biases or preconceptions that prevent you from seeing group interactions clearly. Do you have any inkling of what some of these biases might be? If so, jot them down. If not, make a mental note to rethink the question as you read more.

NOTES

1. I am indebted to the following book for insight into historical management evolution: Claudes George, Jr., *The History of Management Thought* (Englewood Cliffs, NJ: Prentice-Hall, 1968).

2. Robert T. Golembiewski, *The Small Group* (Chicago: University of Chicago Press, 1962), pp. 1-2.

3. Fred L. Strodbeck, "The Case for the Study of Small Groups," *American Sociological Review* 29 (1954): 651.

4. H. C. Metcalf and L. Urwick, *Dynamic Administration: The Collected Papers of Mary Parker Follet* (New York: Harper, 1924).

5. F. J. Roethlisberger and W. J. Dixon, *Management and the Worker* (Cambridge: Harvard University Press, 1939).

6. L. Coch and J. R. P. French, "Overcoming Resistance to Change," *Human Relations* 1 (1948): 512-32. See also Alfred J. Marrow, *The Practical Theorist: The Life and Work of Kurt Lewin* (New York: Basic Books, 1969); Muzafer Sherif et al., *Intergroup Conflict and Cooperation: The Robber's Cave Experiment* (Norman, OK: Book Exchange, 1961).

7. Leland P. Bradford, Jack R. Gibb, and Kenneth D. Benne, *T-Group Theory and Laboratory Method* (New York: Wiley, 1964); William B. Eddy and Bernard Lubin, "Laboratory Training and Encounter Groups," *Personnel and Guidance Journal* 49 (1971): 625-34.

8. Golembiewski, *The Small Group*. See also George C. Homans, *The Human Group* (New York: Harcourt, Brace and World, 1950); Dorwin Cartwright and Alvin Zander, eds., *Group Dynamics: Research and Theory*, 3d ed. (Evanston, IL: Row, Peterson and Company, 1968).

9. Rensis Likert, *New Patterns in Management* (New York: McGraw-Hill, 1961).

10. Erich Trist and K. W. Banford, "Some Group and Psychological Consequences of the Long Wall Method of Coal Getting," *Human Relations* 4 (1951): 3-38; A. T. Wilson, "Some Aspects of Social Process," *Journal of Social Issues* 5 (1951): 5-23.

11. Robert R. Blake and Jane S. Mouton, *Group Dynamics: Key to Decision-Making* (Houston, TX: Gulf Publishing Company, 1961).

12. Jay Hall, "Decisions, Decisions, Decisions," *Psychology Today* 5 (1971): 51-54, 86-88.

13. John K. Galbraith, *The New Industrial State*, 2d ed., rev. (Boston: Houghton Mifflin, 1971).

14. Chris Argyris, "Today's Problems with Tomorrow's Organizations," *Journal of Management Studies* 4 (1967): 31-55. Reprinted in *Behavioral Science and the Manager's Role*, W. B. Eddy and W. W. Burke, eds. (LaJolla, CA: University Associates, 1980).

2

HUMAN FACTORS IN GROUPS: WHAT MEMBERS BRING WITH THEM

Joe Harkens mentally surveyed his committee as he waited for the meeting to begin. "How can a collection of individuals, each working for the same organization, see things so differently and react in such different ways?" He mused, "I wonder what they want from this group? I'd like to know if there's any way of getting them to pull together once in a while!"

A significant proportion of what happens in a group stems directly or indirectly from the individual characteristics of the members—their past experience, their values, their needs and goals, and aspects of their current lives. It is a mistake to underestimate these influences and operate as though members have entered the group fresh and new, uncontaminated by previous experiences. Perhaps the first key to effective group leadership is the ability to understand and appreciate each member in her or his unique individuality. There is a vast body of literature on human behavior. Unfortunately, it is not synthesized into a concise picture—far from it! Thus we cannot, in the space available, make you an expert. What we can do, however, is highlight some of the aspects of behavior, with attention to those areas that bear most directly on our goal of understanding working groups.

DILEMMAS IN INDIVIDUAL–GROUP RELATIONS

Before delving into specific principles of behavior, a few problem areas in understanding individuals in groups need to be dealt with. There are three issues which, if not clarified, can confuse thinking about groups. These are the belief in a group mind, conformity versus individuality, and the myth of rationality.

The Group Mind

There is an old argument about whether a group is something greater than, or different from, the sum of its parts. To people who work with groups it sometimes seems that when a number of individuals come together to work and interact closely for a period of time, something almost magical happens. The group seems to become an entity in its own right, with a personality separate from those of the individual members. Members' behavior in the group seems to be different from their actions outside it. Earlier students of groups sometimes used the term *group mind* to denote such a phenomenon, particularly when it referred to the behavior of a large collection of people, such as a mob. Such mystification of groups is not very useful. Group behavior is the combination and interaction (though not the simple sum) of all the members—with their characteristic styles and past experiences—in concert with the group's task, its history, its resources, and other aspects of the setting.

Some groups develop high degrees of excitement, cross-fertilization of ideas, mutual encouragement, and achievement. The term *synergy* has been used to describe an atmosphere that calls forth the best from the members. It may foster learning, self-confidence, and increased motivation, in which case the members' best effort may be even better than it was before they joined the group. Or, conversely, the atmosphere generated in group interaction may be so negative, sterile, or punitive that members tend to perform far below their potential. These differences in climate are explainable by the behavior of the members, and in turn further affect the members' performance. The question, "Which came first, member behavior or group climate?" would be a chicken-and-egg dilemma except for the fact that members of working groups have acquired most of their behavioral tendencies long before experiencing the climate of their present groups. (It is true, of course, that the climate of our most basic group, the family, had a profound influence on our attitudes and behaviors.)

Is Individuality Possible?

A related problem has to do with group pressure on the individual to conform. There is no question that groups sometimes do act in ways that override the wishes of some of their members. This is particularly true in groups in which the leader (or leaders) are autocratic and enforce procedures that make individual expression of opinions difficult or risky. It is also true of groups in which there is a conflict or significant split in opinion. In such cases the majority subgroup (possibly including the leader) may act to suppress the behavior of a minority subgroup or single dissenter. Thus, members face a dilemma. They wish to meet their individual needs and to express their feelings; but they run the risk of being pressured into conformity. If they need to retain their membership for any reason (to keep their job, because the boss appointed them, they need the support of the group, etc.) they then find themselves in a serious conflict between two sets of needs. Some individuals make the decision to stifle their own tendencies and to conform to group norms. Often they pay a price in poor morale or increased stress. Others may elect to leave the group in search of a better climate.

Irving Janis has studied social conformity in groups and identified a process of suppression of dissent, which he refers to as *groupthink*. In a penetrating analysis that should be read by everyone who works with groups, Janis describes how pressures for conformity may overrule critical and logical thinking. In some groups, norms develop that favor comfort, avoidance of conflict, and adherence to the "party line" at all costs. These norms may be a result of the leadership, the history of the group, or pressures from outside. Deviance in the form of disagreement, questioning of established patterns, or injection of new information or ideas is looked on with disfavor. Concurrence is valued and rewarded; cohesiveness is preserved at all cost. Under these conditions, input from members that could help avoid costly mistakes, break new ground, or correct wrong directions is stifled in subtle or not so subtle ways, and the group suffers in the long run.[1]

Janis cites the Kennedy administration's Bay of Pigs debacle as a classic example of groupthink. There were those in the administration who strongly believed that both the information and the logic supporting the proposed invasion were faulty. But the climate of the group discussions was such that those who favored the invasion were in control and dissent was discouraged. Janis quotes Arthur Schlesinger, one of the dissenters, who wrote, "I can only explain my failure to do more than raise a few timid questions by reporting that one's impulse to blow the whistle on this nonsense was simply undone by the circumstances of the discussion."

The Myth of Pure Rationality

In modern society, embued as it is with science, reason, and rationality, we sometimes make the incorrect assumption that we can separate our feelings from our behavior. Some groups and some leaders create a set of implicit or explicit norms (rules and/or expectations) such that when members come to the group they should, to paraphrase the old song, "leave their feelings on the doorstep." This is impossible; the expectation is inherently frustrating. Our emotions (including anger and fear), attitudes, needs, values, and goals are as much a part of us as is our physiology. We participate in groups as whole persons, not as space-age cyborgs, half machine and half human that can shut off the emotional subsystem. Our feelings affect our behavior in groups, whether or not they are accepted as legitimate and whether we like it or not. The leader who admonishes, "Let's keep feelings out of it," may either not understand the realities of human group behavior or be uneasy with emotional issues in groups. The evidence is more than ample that human emotions that are denied expression in group settings "go underground" and find expression in more subtle and often more destructive ways. For example, in a group I worked with members were not allowed to express their concerns or ideas. One day they were asked to comment on a proposal presented by the leader. They vented their hostility in passive–aggressive ways by not pointing out the serious flaws they saw in the proposal, waiting with inward glee for the leader's plan to fail. A useful principle is to help the group deal with emotional issues in such a way that those issues do not block progress later on.

In summary, group behavior is a result of the complex interaction of the members and is affected by their past experience, emotions, interactive styles, needs, and goals. Member behavior is also influenced by factors present in the group, such as leadership style and nature of the task. The next section begins the process of describing the various aspects of human behavior relevant to group operations.

THE PERSONAL PERSPECTIVE

If ten of us come together to form a team, there are, in an important sense, ten group realities rather than one. Each member perceives and responds to the situation from his or her own individual perspective. No two members see and hear things quite the same way. Each one comes with different needs and purposes; every member reacts emotionally somewhat differently than others. Thus, each member participates in the group and evaluates the experience from the point of view of his/her own subjective perspective.

Carlos Castenada, a student of anthropology, entered into apprenticeship with the old Indian sorcerer Don Juan.[2] A major part of Castaneda's learning process involved episodes in which he experienced the world in entirely new and startling ways. For example, his teacher performed feats for which no explanation existed within his own knowledge framework, such as leaping to great heights. Castaneda was surprised to learn that there are *different realities*, and that his usual way of perceiving the world is only one of many possible ways. Even though Don Juan's magic made the separation of realities more dramatic, perhaps Castaneda should not have been so surprised. Each of us exists in our own separate reality. Each has a unique perspective. I cannot expect you to experience things the same way I do. You cannot expect me to react as you react. One step toward greater understanding of group member's behavior is to get a firm grasp on the fact that each person responds from his or her own distinct reality.

The leader who says "The objectives of this group are perfectly clear and straightforward. There's no reason for disagreement. Let's move on," is making unwarranted assumptions about individual differences. So is the member who says, "This memo really makes me mad! I can't understand why the rest of you aren't angry too! You must not care." And so is the member who says, "There's no reason to be tense and upset. Look at me, I'm perfectly calm."

It is usually not necessary, of course, to settle for realities that are far apart. Efforts to understand private realities and bring them closer together are often helpful in groups and relationships. An

Indian adage advocated walking a mile in the other person's moccasins. Social scientists use the term empathy. Both imply putting yourself in the place of the other person and looking at the world from his or her perspective. Group time devoted to exploring members' differing views and feelings about important factors is often time well spent.

Implications of the above for working with groups are: (1) never assume that group members will see or hear things the same way, (2) never expect members to react to an idea or event the same way, (3) don't be in too big a hurry to assign right/wrong evaluations to differences, and (4) time spent exploring differences in the spirit of achieving greater understanding can narrow the gaps between members' realities and bring about smoother operations.

Another technique for overcoming differences is to help members find a common ground. If they are seeking the same or similar goals they will be motivated to resolve differences. If they share interests, values, or concerns, these can be weighed against factors that separate them.

SELF-CONCEPT AND SELF-ESTEEM

One of the most important aspects of each of our own realities is our view of ourselves. A person's self-concept lies at the very base of his or her own style of interaction with others. Most of us will go to great lengths to preserve our concept of ourselves, and threats to our self-concept may bring about defensiveness, stress, and resistance to change.

The process of learning who we are is a crucial aspect of our humanity. The basic nature of our self-concept begins forming when we are very young, and has been developing and changing ever since. It comes from our inteactions with other people and elements in the environment. Sociologist Charles Coley used the term "looking-glass self" to suggest that we are defined to a significant degree by the image of us reflected by other people. Based on past experience (including messages from our parents), all of us have a preferred self-image that we believe represents the best side of us. We are willing to go to almost any length to preserve that self-image and present it to others because its preservation enhances our self-esteem. Anything that tarnishes our self-image and diminishes our self-esteem is met with defensiveness and avoided, if possible.

The self-concept serves to ground us in our own reality. It helps us understand how we are different from parents and others around us, and it provides us with an identity. A common fear is that others will not perceive us in ways that are consonant with our self-concept. We seek out others to validate our self-perceptions. Yet if we are not seen in ways in which we see ourselves (or in ways we wish to be seen), we risk disconfirmation and loss of self-esteem. These are unpleasant and stress-producing experiences.

It should be clear why issues related to self-image and the need to maintain self-esteem are significant in groups. Members bring with them a human tendency to preserve a positive image. Most of us, as we participate in a group, are concerned at some level with questions like, "How am I seen by others? Will I be accepted? Will I be able to carry some influence in the group? What kind of role should I play?" Furthermore, most (though not all) of us entertain some doubts about whether others, if they *really* knew our true selves, would like and accept us. So we develop the habit of putting on acts or "wearing a mask." We may present an image somewhat different from our true nature and feelings in an attempt to create the image we desire. We may act relaxed and confident and all-knowing even though inside we are tense and confused. We may attempt to come across as fearless and aggressive when we are really afraid. We may treat the leader with deference and respect, though our real attitude is one of dislike. And we may bluff when we don't know anything about the subject.

Members' needs to preserve their self-concept and avoid disconfirmation pose several problems for groups. One problem is that in early stages of groups, members may experience significant concerns (often unspoken) about identity and self-image. They may have difficulty settling down to the task at hand and forgetting about their discomfort until they have eased these concerns. They may be asking themselves, "Who are these other people? What are their backgrounds and qualifications? How do I stack up? Is this a risky situation? Am I likely to be criticized or ridiculed for expressing my views?" Most members, if asked bluntly, would laughingly deny these concerns, and indeed they might be largely unaware of them. Their existence, however, is well documented. For example, in many training groups I have worked with, members are able, after a good deal of training and practice, to look back at their early concerns and discuss them. They are almost invariably surprised that many others in the group had the same concerns. Everyone had concealed them in order to preserve the self-image. The reader might usefully ask, "What concerns go through my mind when I move into a new group, especially when I am not the leader or when I'm not sure how my qualifications compare with those of others?"

Many good leaders devote some time in initial stages of groups (or when new members enter) to the process of getting acquainted. Members may be asked to introduce themselves, say where they are from, what they did before joining the group, etc. Such techniques are helpful, but are often performed too quickly or superficially. Time spent (within reason) gaining greater understanding of who is in the group is usually a good investment in group productivity.

Another problem with self-image has to do with difficulties caused by incongruence between actual feelings and behavior. When people act out roles and attempt to present ideally perfect selves, they use up an undue amount of their energy and internal resources maintaining the discrepancy between what is going on inside and what they are doing on the outside. Also, the information that is being fed into the group's work activity may be distorted or incomplete because of members' need to look good, cover up bad news, flatter the leader, act important, etc.

The problem of self-image and self-protection can be eased if members develop high levels of trust and confidence in each other and in the leader. Under these conditions it is possible for members to function with much less need to maintain their defenses. They may also learn more about how their view of themselves compares with others' views, thus reducing another source of concern. Approaches to raising group trust levels and encouraging constructive feedback will be discussed later. The closing point here is a reminder to the manager that group members are greatly concerned about preserving their self-image and self-esteem. If the situation is threatening they will play-act (often without being aware of it) to the point of altering the way they participate in the group and the impact they make. This means that in groups in which members feel threatened and defensive, energy is being used up on self-protection and the communication is likely to be contaminated by strategizing, posturing, or withdrawing.

HUMAN NEEDS IN GROUP SETTINGS

It is customary in psychology to divide the study of behavior into the categories of motivation, perception, and learning/thinking/

problem solving. We will follow this convention for a brief survey of some behavioral principles relevant to understanding people in groups.

Central to the study of human behavior in any setting is the issue of motivation. Most observers will readily acknowledge that humans are striving, goal-seeking creatures, and that the mainspring that drives us seems to be a set of needs or desires that propel us toward those things we want and away from those we dislike or fear. The study of motivation is complex; because we cannot observe motives or needs directly, we can only observe a person's behavior and infer from it something about its causes.

At the most basic level, individuals make decisions about whether to remain in the group or leave it by weighing the benefits and costs of membership. They may seek out membership in a new committee because they feel such membership would give them some desired rewards or be an improvement over their existing situations. Or, when assigned to a particular group, they may accept the assignment (as opposed to protesting or being absent or quitting) because they decide to avoid the negative costs. They may work hard to retain membership in a group that is rewarding for them, and either leave the group or cease productive membership (psychologically quitting) when the negative factors outweigh the positive.[3]

Analysis of human motivation in groups is important because it helps us understand what members want to get from their participation, why they strive for the things they do, and what outcomes are likely to cause satisfaction or dissatisfaction. There are a variety of different theories and models that seek to explain motivation and it is impossible to cover them all here. We focus here on a few basic principles of motivation which, when taken together, provide a picture of that aspect of group behavior that stems from the needs and drives of members.

ERG Theory

Clayton Alderfer has developed a theory of motivation that is particularly applicable to behavior in organizational and group settings. The view is similar to the need hierarchy proposed by the late Abraham Maslow, but is research based and somewhat more straightforward. Alderfer divides human needs into the three categories of existence, relatedness, and growth.[4]

Existence needs encompass a person's basic physiological and material desires: food, pay, working conditions, physical comfort, and safety.

Relatedness needs focus on relationships with other people and involve the interchange of thoughts and feelings.

Growth needs are responsible for a person's effort to learn new capabilities, to create, and to develop new aspects of his or her personality.

One can assume that most of the goal-seeking activity observed among group members fits into one of the three need categories, or perhaps into two overlapping categories. For example, reasons for joining the group or organization in the first place may involve existence needs (desire for income, security, physical effort, etc.). If the member finds the satisfaction of these needs threatened, he or she may act to protect the security of his/her membership. Thus it is one of the criticisms of bureaucracy that many people expend their energy at the existence level, protecting their job security and continued membership, rather than taking the risks involved in creativity and change.

Relatedness needs come into direct play in group interactions. Individuals have intensive and complex need systems in the area of relationships with others, and these are played out in group situations. Even though they may believe they are completely task oriented and free of interpersonal concerns, most members are strongly influenced in their work together by their relatedness needs. Strengths and kinds of relatedness needs vary among individuals, depending on past learning and levels of satisfaction in contemporary life. Some common relatedness needs in group settings include the following:

• The need to establish supportive relationships in which people can share their thoughts and feelings with each other;

• The need to "be heard" and understood on significant matters and to find others who will respond with genuine interest and concern when we express ourselves;

• The need to feel a sense of acceptance and belonging, to be liked by others;

• The need to receive confirmation from others as a significant and worthwhile person;

• The need to maintain some degree of influence or power in interactions, to exert leadership.

Members may bring growth needs into the group with them, and may expect to meet such needs either as a primary or secondary aspect of their participation. For example, they may expect to develop new skills and competencies as a result of their participation, they may hope to enhance their leadership abilities, or they may desire to have new and different experiences. As in the other need areas, levels of growth needs vary from individual to individual, but most competent members will not be content to participate for long in groups in which there are no possibilities for growth.

Growth needs may play a major role in some groups and a lesser role in others. The behavioral sciences have, over the past three decades, developed training groups whose purpose is human growth and development. These include sensitivity training groups, therapy groups, and conference and workshop groups focused on helping members further their personal development by learning more about themselves and testing out new behaviors.[5]

In Alderfer's theory, the three types of needs are assumed to progress from lower (existence) to higher (growth) needs. Considerable research effort has gone into exploring the relationships among the three need categories. The complete findings are too numerous and complex to document completely here. However, generally, whenever a need is not satisfied, the desire for it and for the need area below it increases in intensity. Thus, when relatedness needs are not satisfied, desire for both existence and relatedness needs increases.

Alderfer suggests an approach to organizational application of his theory and findings that is highly relevant to groups. The kinds of satisfaction that are available to a person in a particular situation will determine the kinds of rewards he/she will seek. If little or no provision is made for the development of relationships that support a satisfying exchange of ideas and feelings, and if material factors are relatively scarce, members will focus on existence and relatedness needs, and most of their energy will go into seeking ways to satisfy these needs. Alderfer calls this condition the *existence–deficiency* cycle. If, on the other hand, the group situation supports satisfying interpersonal relationships and opportunity for members to develop their capacities, a *growth–enrichment* cycle is encouraged and members will tend to focus on growth and development. This view of member motivation provides a challenge to every group leader to work toward a climate that supports growth and minimizes obsession with safety and comfort.

Expectation Theory

Another element of human motivation deals with the role played in motivation by people's expectations. This tool for understanding behavior is not the result of the writing of any single individual, but has been formulated from the work of a number of experimental and industrial psychologists.[6]

Simply stated, goals that people seek for satisfaction and conditions that they attempt to escape in order to avoid dissatisfaction are not absolute, but are based in part on expectations. Expectations are a result of the interaction between needs and lessons from past experiences. I may enter into a group with the goal of being perceived as the foremost expert on the topic being discussed. In this case my expectation level leads me to set a high level of performance and recognition for myself. I will be disappointed if my rather lofty goal is not attained. You may come to the group knowing that the discussion topic is new for you, and hoping only that you can learn a little and get by without being embarrassed. When you learn that you are able to participate in the discussion as capably as many of the others, you will be pleased to have exceeded your expectation level and fared no worse than average. Thus, our reactions to what happens to us depend on the discrepancy (or lack of it) between what we expect and what actually happens.

A variety of factors may influence a group member's expectations about the potential for rewards and the likelihood of unpleasant experience. General attitudes about groups in the organization (whether they are valued or belittled), selection procedures used to determine membership, announcements sent out prior to meetings, the group leader's reputation, and the member's interest in the work or subject of the group are all factors that may affect participation. Effective group leaders both understand and influence the expectations of their members. What do members expect when they first come to the group, and what can be done to assure that these expectations are accurate reflections of what actually will happen? Clues to unmet expectations may arise during discussion. A statement like, "This is not what I thought we would be doing," "I'd heard that this group works on bigger problems than this," or "When can we discuss rewriting our goals and objectives?" should tip off the leader that an exploration of expectations is in order.

Summary of Motivational Influences

It is now possible to combine the theories described above into a concise (though incomplete) view of group member motivation. People join and participate in groups with the expectation of satisfying one or more of their needs in the categories of existence, relatedness, and growth. If membership in the group means primarily keeping one's job and paying the bills, then existence needs are dominant. Other aspects of existence needs may arise over the course of the group's operation (the need for physical comfort, food, safety from threat, etc.). Group members may compete for scarce resources related to existence needs (money, materials, space).

Individuals who are not compelled to spend all their time and energy struggling to exist come into groups with the hope of satisfying the relatedness needs they bring with them. They hope to participate in interactions with others which provide support, recognition, respect, and friendship. Or they may wish to acquire rewards that will earn them esteem and positive feelings about themselves both inside and outside the group. They probably also hope to avoid being rejected, excluded, or disliked. Specific kinds of relatedness needs and their intensity vary from one individual to another. However, there are very few people who have no needs for relatedness (although they may not understand these needs in themselves or deny their existence in order to avoid the risk of embarrassment).

It is crucial for the leader to recognize that relatedness needs are an integral part of every person. In brief and infrequent meetings it is possible that a highly structured and impersonal procedure can override relatedness needs. In working groups or other long-term or intensive settings, it is virtually impossible to function without their intrusion. Unsatisfied relatedness needs can not simply be ignored and forgotten. When relatedness needs are frustrated, the person's desire for and efforts toward satisfying them instensify.

As relatedness needs become relatively satisfied, growth needs become a greater source of motivation. Individuals seek to help create situations in which they can increase their skills, learn new things, play different roles, try out new ways of functioning. Group members may express concerns about being in a rut, always doing things the same way, and feeling the need to bring in fresh ideas and perspectives. They may push to have greater time and resources made available for learning and development. And they may even leave to go to other situations that provide greater opportunities for growth.

A particular individual's response to a group situation depends on (a) the strength of his/her various needs in the categories of existence, relatedness, and growth; (b) the potential of the situation to satisfy those needs; and (c) the expectations the individual brings into the group about what needs he or she will be likely to satisfy. Thus we may, for example, picture a 60-year-old supervisor who has a low level of relatedness needs (either because those needs are satisfied in other areas of his life, or because that need area is not strong for him) who is appointed to membership on the plant safety committee. He (as well as the other old hands) has very low expectations for any interesting participation in this group, because the safety director runs it as a rubber-stamp group. As long as meetings are not too physically uncomfortable or inconvenient, the supervisor will probably derive neither significant satisfaction or dissatisfaction. He is likely to act responsibly (because membership is a part of his job), but he will also tend to be fairly passive.

Contrast this situation with membership on the same committee by a new young management trainee with a need to learn and grow in the company, a desire to relate to others in the plant, and the expectation (based on college personnel courses) that the committee can be an effective participative body that makes significant strides in reducing accidents. The same conditions are perceived and reacted to quite differently because of differences in the needs and expectations of the two men. The effective group leader makes every effort to diagnose member needs and expectations early in the group's life (or even before it is formed, if possible). Such a diagnosis can be an informal process of talking with participants about what they want and expect from the group, or it can involve more formal measurement through questionnaires or interviews.

Self-Oriented Behavior

Sometimes people bring into a group needs or motives that influence their behavior in ways that seem inappropriate, disruptive, or deviant. They seem to be responding to what is going on inside themselves rather than to activities in the group. This condition has been labeled self-oriented behavior. One individual may seem inordinately frightened and shy, more so than any realistic appraisal of the situation would seem to dictate. Another might talk incessantly, interrupting and ignoring others and hampering the ability of the group to do its work. One person may clown and show off, and in other ways draw discussion away from the topic and to himself. Still another might be unusually quick to vent angry comments at others for seemingly minor irritations. These individuals are said by clinicians to be acting out, that is, they are unconsciously acting out in the present situation old fears, needs, and other emotional experiences from their earlier lives. While it is certainly true that all of us, to one degree or another, carry our past concerns into the present, self-oriented behavior is a particular problem for groups because it often disrupts normal interaction.

While one does not want to be too quick to label a dissenting member self-oriented (and thus discount him or her), it is important to recognize such characteristics. Self-oriented members pose a problem for both the leader and the other members. Logic often does not work to reduce their disruptive behavior. Indeed, they may not recognize their behavior as deviant, or may not admit it. Many of us are intimidated by emotionally inappropriate behavior and pretend to ignore it (except to talk about the individual outside the group). The first steps in dealing with deviant or self-oriented individuals are to hear them out, to express the value of opposing points of view, and to provide support. If the behavior continues to be damaging to the group's overall functioning, and if diplomatic suggestions and normal group pressures do not bring about necessary modifications, the leader may be well advised to consult an outside resource person trained to handle such problems.[7]

PERCEPTION: GATHERING INFORMATION
ABOUT THE INNER AND OUTER REALITIES

It is customary for books about the psychology of organizational behavior to contain a section on perception. In these cases perception refers to a much broader aspect of the person than is tested when one goes to the optometrist for a vision check. Perception deals with processes whereby the individual gathers information about the world in which he or she lives. It involves the five senses (plus possibly some others that we do not yet understand) and the internal mechanisms that interpret the data derived from these senses and give it meaning. The meaning that any event or object carries for us has to do with past experiences, the ways we have learned to categorize or classify what we perceive, and our system of needs. Thus what we see is a combination of what is really out there and the meaning we attach to it. It isn't surprising that two people observing a complex phenomenon often perceive very different things.

Psychologists have developed useful information about perception in organizations. Zalkind and Costello summarize findings pertinent to administrators.[8] Others such as Leavitt have added their ideas.[9] Much of this information is directly relevant to group situations. Some general findings:

• We tend to perceive best those things that are positive and desirable and confirm our viewpoint. We tend to miss or ignore those things that are negative, disconfirming, and undesirable unless they clearly indicate imminent danger. This process is called *selective perception*. Members who find conflict unpleasant and threatening, for example, may not be aware of indicators of group animosity and emotion that others easily identify. They tend to be the ones who say, "I don't think Mary is really angry, she's just doing that for effect."

• We tend to use pre-established categories into which we put people in order to more easily and quickly decide how to deal with them. Some such stereotypes may be valid and helpful in some group situations. ("Harry seems to be one of those quiet people who often require support and encouragement in order to participate in discussions.") Or they can be invalid, bigoted, and destructive. ("Sally has a Polish last name. I don't even have to wait for her to speak to know what kind of person she is.")

• We use the term *opinion* to denote things about the world that a person believes to be factually true because he or she has perceived them directly or indirectly. ("Groups of more than 15 are hard to manage; conflict is best resolved by having the leader decide between the two opposing positions.") Attitudes are opinions that include emotional and evaluative components.[10] ("People who get into authority positions are manipulative and should be distrusted; women should not be allowed in this group because they are talkative and not task oriented.") Most of us are susceptible to believing that we hold opinions based on facts and that other people hold attitudes that are distorted with emotional biases.

• The views and positions of people around us influence our perceptions. Studies have demonstrated that many of us actually begin to see things differently when we find ourselves at odds with important people. This social pressure acts to bring divergent views into line with the majority. My students who graduate and seek work in corporations at first change their clothing styles in order to gain acceptance. In a few months, however, most will actually perceive their new mode of dress as more appropriate and attractive than jeans. The popular music that my teenage children listen to sounds uninteresting and repetitive to me. Predictably, the pop music from my teenage years sounds uninteresting and repetitive to them. Peer group views of popular music act to legitimate and support perceptual differences between parents and children.

• Groups exert social pressure, often unconsciously, in order to reduce the tension of divergence. The danger of such pressure is that it may rob the group of unpopular but important viewpoints, detract from creativity, and give the leader a false sense of agreement. We are frequently unaware of the ways in which our perceptions become influenced and distorted by our emotions and habits. Our need to maintain a positive self-image (including the belief that our perceptions are accurate) and to eliminate internal dissonance sometimes lead us to trust the accuracy of our perceptions too much. Most of us have been involved in endless group arguments about whose view of some piece of the world (such as the quality of a football team) is valid. Often we get involved in a right/wrong dilemma, with each party unable to believe that the other could possibly see things as they do, unless they're blind or stupid, or both.

If there is an overriding principle, it is that the emotions (including needs, attitudes, and motives) affect perception. Effective group leadership requires careful attention to the dangers of perceptual distortion. Periodic checks to explore the similarities and differences in the way members are perceiving things can be useful. So can training, which helps members understand their perceptual differences.

Finally, accurate self-perception is the trickiest quest of all. Whatever problems I may have perceiving the world accurately are multiplied when I try to get an unbiased picture of myself in my group leadership role. Not only do my own self-image, my need for self-esteem, and my other needs and attitudes get in the way, but other group members, especially if they work for me or fear me, are very likely to collude by telling me what they think I want to hear. This is why many managers go to training programs outside the company to interact with strangers (who have nothing to gain by withholding information), or conduct anonymous attitude surveys or hire consultants. As we indicated earlier in the chapter, a clear and accurate self-concept is an essential ingredient of successful leadership.

LEARNING

Groups are expected to solve problems by pooling their expertise. Members are selected because they have knowledge and skills relevant to the problem or task at hand. Thus, a group charged with designing a better mousetrap would no doubt want members who know about mice and traps and perhaps even cheese. The assumption is that the more experience and knowledge available about the problem to be solved, the better the problem solving. This is logical, except that often groups fail to solve problems, not because they don't bring in enough information about the subject, but because they don't have the skills to work together effectively. Functioning well within a group involves a particular set of skills, just as surely as does analyzing a firm's financial situation or performing an experiment in a chemistry laboratory.

The third area of behavior to be explored is that of learning, including thinking and problem solving. In effective ongoing groups members do not remain static in their knowledge and understanding. The group should provide the stimulus and opportunity for each member to learn about: (1) the subject matter or business of the group, (i.e., the Jones Project, problems in the personnel department, policies for software acquisitions, etc.); (2) skills for more effective group participation; (3) the people in the group, including oneself. As we indicated earlier in this chapter, growth needs are a part of the human motivational system and are most active in groups that have been able to satisfy more basic needs. The leader's challenge is to respond to members' needs to learn and grow, and to the group's need for increasing problem-solving knowledge and skill by creating a climate that supports learning.

There are two hurdles in providing people with better group leadership and membership skills. One is that many of us believe we already know what we need to know. After all, we have been interacting with others all our lives. The other hurdle is that some people believe that effective group functioning doesn't really involve learnable skills. They think it has more to do with being comfortable with people and/or smart enough to figure out how to get your way. The fact is that some of us were lucky enough to grow up in a family or other early life situation in which the ways of interacting we learned gave us good basic preparation for working well in groups. We gained good *interpersonal competence.* Others of us were not so lucky. Instead of learning good interpersonal skills we learned inappropriate or dysfunctional ways of behaving. In truth, of course, most of us have carried forth from our interpersonal learning some helpful skills and some non-helpful habits and styles. It is also true that there is a good deal more to learn about management in group situations than earlier experience has provided any of us.

Students of human learning have generated extensive research and theory to explain what learning is, and why and how it occurs. There are several schools of thought that offer different explanations. For our purposes, it is sufficient to say that learning involves a change in behavior (either actual or potential) as a result of experience. Learning is activated through motivation. We learn a new idea or piece of information or skill because it has some value to us and/or is accompanied by positive feelings. Thus we learn to ride a bicycle, write our name, speak in public, or like ice cream cones. Learning also results from a need to avoid punishing or painful experiences (not to touch a hot stove, talk back to the teacher, or criticize the boss). However, the learning that results from threat or punishment is often less predictable and more likely to be accompanied by troublesome side effects than is positively reinforced learning. It is also true that people often do not learn because they do not know that information is available that could be useful to them. For example, the attitudes and techniques in "defensive driving" are more likely to be learned if one knows about the concept and its utility in preventing accidents.

Questions for group leaders are: (1) What do my group members need to learn (what do I think and what do they think they need to learn); (2) How can I make available opportunities and information for learning?; (3) What will motivate members to learn?; (4) How can I help create a climate that supports and encourages growth and development? Although there is no formula that resolves these issues for all groups, there are some guidelines derived from the fields of training and adult education.

Learning often requires effort and members may not expend the energy unless they see it meeting some of their needs. The manager can begin by setting the tone. Demonstrating an active interest in his or her own learning is the place to start. Discussing expectations about members' learning and its value to group performance are also beneficial. Creating learning opportunities is the next step. Training programs, reading materials, group discussions, field trips and other educational resources provide the substance of the learning. A key consideration should always be to relate the ongoing activities and needs of the group.

Adult educator Malcolm Knowles has provided useful insight into how adults, in contrast to children, go about learning. Adults are more self-directed. They seek out learning opportunities that they believe will be useful to them in solving a problem or meeting a need. Adults are interested in applications—they want practical and useful learning. They often bring a great deal of experience and expertise into the learning situation, and expect to utilize that experience. (It is also true that some past lessons may be dysfunctional in that they may be invalid or inhibiting in the new situations. In that case, adult learning becomes, in part, a matter of unlearning and relearning.)[11]

Donald Schon has used the term "learning system" to describe how organizations need to function to remain viable in an unstable environment. The concept applies equally well to groups. Most groups in complex organizations or communities operate in ambiguous, changing environments. This means that goals, limitations, interface resources, and membership do not remain static. Established practices from the past often do not work. In order to maintain viability, the group itself often needs to become a "learning system"; that is, it must: pursue as a major part of its functioning a continuing effort to sense changes in its environment, devise innovations that improve adaptation to new conditions, gain new information and knowledge, and open itself up to changes in role, scope, and boundaries.[12]

CONCLUSION

Kurt Lewin, a pioneer in applied group theory, used the formula $B = f(P + S)$ to indicate that *B*ehavior is a function of the interaction of the *P*erson and the *S*ituation. This chapter has sought to provide a brief overview of some of the aspects of the *P*erson that manifest themselves in significant ways in groups. We have noted that in order to understand people we need to look at them (and ourselves) from all aspects, not just the rational, thinking side emphasized in business settings. We have discussed the need to protect self-esteem and self-image. We have viewed human motivation and discussed how basic needs combine with expectations and situational characteristics to structure goals and satisfactions. We have looked at the processes of perception and have seen how many factors contribute to the image we see. And finally, we have separated interpersonal skills from task skills and have looked at one schema to illustrate the qualities of effective interpersonal relations.

We have seen that individuals enter a group bringing with them a good deal of baggage. Their psychological makeup stems from past experiences and parental teaching and includes motives, perceptions, and expectations. In the next chapter we will discuss another set of baggage that members carry into a new group—the attitudes and values from the culture in which they live.

LEARNING AIDS

1a. Where do you, personally, stand on the question of group conformity versus individuality? Do you feel comfortable giving up some of your ability to act independently in return for a group's aid and stimulation, or do you resent the time and energy you expend in groups? Place yourself on the scale below:

1 2 3 4	5 6 7	8 9 10
High individuality	Medium individuality	High conformity
Low conformity	Medium conformity	Low individuality

1b. Rate the person(s) you interact most frequently with in groups on the same scale.

2. In this chapter we discussed the fact that each member experiences the group from the point of view of his or her own personal perspective or "reality." Identify a situation in which members' different perspectives caused difficulties in your group.

3. Select one of the groups you identified in Chapter 1 and do an assessment of its "need satisfaction potential" using ERG theory. That is, what specific need satisfiers in the categories of existence, relatedness, and growth is the group likely to be able to provide?

Existence needs _____

Relatedness needs _____

Growth needs _____

4. In a group in which you are member or leader conduct a discussion of member needs and expectations.
   A. Ask members to write down individually and then discuss the expectations they had when they entered the group. What needs (hopes, interests, desires) did they want the group to fulfill?
   B. What are their frustrations (what needs have not been fulfilled?).
   C. What might the group do to better meet the needs of its members?

5. Ask group members to list and discuss the following:
   A. What are some of the major similarities and differences among group members?
   B. In what ways are these similarities and differences likely to enhance group creativity and in what ways are they likely to cause conflict?

NOTES

1. Irving Janis, "Groupthink" *Psychology Today*, 5, 6 (Nov. 1971): 43–46 & 74–76. Also see his *Victims of Groupthink* (Atlanta: Houghton Mifflin, 1972).

2. Carlos Castaneda, *A Separate Reality* (New York: Simon and Schuster, 1971).

3. This "economic" view of group participation is presented by John W. Thibault, and H. H. Kelley in *The Social Psychology of Groups* (New York: Wiley, 1959).

4. Clayton Alderfer, *Existence, Relatedness and Growth: Human Needs in Organizational Settings* (New York: Free Press, 1972).

5. William B. Eddy and Bernard Lubin, "Laboratory Training and Encounter Groups," *Personnel and Guidance Journal* 49 (1971): 625–34.

6. See, for example, David A. Nadler and E. E. Lawler III, "Motivation: A Diagnostic Approach" in *Perspectives on Behavior in Organizations*, J. R. Hackman, E. E. Lawler III, and L. W. Porter, eds. (New York: McGraw-Hill, 1977), pp. 26–38.

7. See Kenneth D. Benne and Paul Sheats, "Functional Roles of Group Members" in *Group Development*, 2d ed., L. P. Bradford, ed. (LaJolla, CA: University Associates, 1978), pp. 52–61.

8. Sheldon S. Zalkind and T. W. Costello, "Perception: Implications for Administration," *Administrative Science Quarterly* 7 (1962): 218–35. Reprinted in H. J. Leavitt and L. R. Pondy, *Readings in Managerial Psychology*, 2d ed. (Chicago: University of Chicago Press, 1964).

9. Harold J. Leavitt, "Perception: From the Inside Looking Out," in *Managerial Psychology*, 4th ed. (Chicago: University of Chicago Press, 1978), Chapter 3.

10. The study of attitudes is a complex subfield in social psychology. See the following for an applied overview: Elliot Aronson, *The Social Animal* (New York: Viking Press, 1972), pp. 85–87.

11. Malcom S. Knowles, *The Adult Learner: A Neglected Species* (Houston, TX: Gulf Publishing Company, 1973).

12. Donald Schon, *Beyond the Stable State* (New York: Norton, 1971).

3

CULTURAL FACTORS: INVISIBLE COMMITTEES AND OTHER MESSAGES FROM THE OUTSIDE

John Burns, director of the hospital pharmacy, had formed a quality circle in his unit. Members of the "QC" met regularly to discuss ways of reducing errors, cutting waste, and improving the work climate. The employees had good ideas about ways to improve the pharmacy, but it was very difficult for the group to get organized and down to business. There were seemingly endless discussions about how the meeting should be conducted. One member, an older pharmacist, felt strongly that the group needed to be highly structured with rules and procedures; younger members wanted things to be looser. Another pharmacist, a graduate of a prestigious university, complained to John that it was inappropriate to include non-pharmacist technicians and clerical personnel in the QC because they lacked professional judgment. Two female technicians with many years of experience tended to hold back and not contribute their thoughts unless asked. A minority group member spent a good deal of time attempting to demonstrate his knowledge and skill. "Why can't these people just sit down and talk with each other as equal human beings?" John wondered. "It seems like they've brought in a pile of excess baggage from their pasts."

CULTURAL VALUES THAT IMPACT ON GROUPS

Central to the operation of any group are questions about what behaviors are appropriate in the setting. No group starts at the beginning when it comes to deciding how to conduct its affairs. When people join a group they bring with them a variety of learned values and standards which have significant impact on how they conduct themselves and how they believe things ought to be done. The culture in which we live, as one of its major functions, provides values and norms (rules) for behavior. Often members have simply accepted cultural values without giving them much thought. These values, though often unspoken, have significant impact on group behavior.

Practitioners of group dynamics have sometimes used the term "invisible committees" to refer to those unseen others who accompany us via our attitudes into groups and influence our behavior. Anyone working with groups can profit from understanding the impact of values on group life. While it is impossible to sort out all the possible invisible committees present, a list of major cultural value issues that are likely to affect most working groups can be devised. The alert leader is likely to find significant expression of the following values in most groups. Differences among group members in their reactions to these values can be sources of misunderstanding and conflict.

Rationality

Western culture has traditionally placed strong emphasis on rational behavior. It has been part of our religious and scientific heritage for hundreds of years to place a positive value on the mind (symbolized by logical analysis and careful rational action) and a negative value on the body, with its unpredictable emotions and drives. Individuals, products of society's educational system, have undergone formal training to perform at a "higher," rational level.

The effects of the norm of rationality are often intensified by a related norm, that of withholding expression of feelings. Many citizens of Western cultures have received strong admonitions to keep their feelings to themselves, especially if they are negative or angry. ("If you can't say something nice, don't say anything at all.") We are taught that it is good to be diplomatic and polite and to avoid conflict, and bad to displease others. Some group members will absorb great amounts of frustration and even leave the group, either psychologically or physically, rather than voice displeasure.

Speculation about why Western civilization has emphasized thinking and de-emphasized feeling has occupied social thinkers for years.

Freud and many others noted the tendency and weighed its advantages and disadvantages. At a very general level, we may say that the Western view has been that the good of civilization depends on our ability to use reasoning, weigh alternatives, plan for the long term, and control destructive or disruptive urges. That it is possible to carry such measures too far is now a fairly well accepted insight.

It should be added that some groups, usually in the therapeutic or training fields, go to the opposite extreme. They downplay the rational aspects of group life and place all the emphasis on expression of feelings. Such a focus is helpful in developing greater understanding of emotional concerns of individuals or within groups. Participants in such experiences may have difficulty adapting to the methodology precisely because of their discomfort in turning loose from an exclusively rational approach.

For the group leader's purpose it is useful to understand the deep pressures for (and sometimes against) rationality that are likely to be present, and to consider the impact of such forces on the work of the group. It is unlikely that a group can maintain viability for long if it ignores or avoids either the social–emotional side or the rational side of its existence. But in seeking an appropriate balance, it will have to deal with deeply entrenched values.

Competition

Most of us in Western cultures receive double messages about competition. On the one hand, it is a desirable and healthy thing. Competing gallantly and successfully enhances one's self-esteem and recognition by demonstrating power and competence. We compete for grades in school, for prizes at parties, and for desirable members of the opposite sex. On the other hand, it is not good form to compete too fiercely, especially against one's peers. Thus, a baseball player is expected to be a "tough competitor" (within the limits of the rules) against rival teams, but not to compete against his own teammates for runs or for popularity. This duality may stem from a conflict between our Judeo-Christian moral tradition and our capitalistic/competitive economic system.

It is common for members of a group who are supposed to be working toward common ends to have competitive feelings toward each other, but to be uncomfortable and covert about the existence of these feelings. They may compete for informal leadership, for recognition by the leader or other high-status members, for a greater share of the discussion time, or for desirable assignments, and yet they may deny their competitiveness, either because they are uncomfortable about its acceptability, or because they want to maintain strategic advantage by not legitimizing competition from others.

It is generally believed that males have traditionally been taught to compete more strongly than have females. Competitive sports are credited with being one of the major sources of teaching. It is now recognized that women are also taught to compete, although in different ways than men. Women tend to compete individually rather than in teams, to be more subtle and to compete more readily with other women.

Like most other cultural value orientations that members bring with them into groups, it is impossible to say whether competitiveness will be helpful or destructive in a particular situation. It depends on the nature of the group and the work it is doing. Probably more often than not, high degrees of competition within a group will lead to wasted time and energy and to frequent outbreaks of conflicts, as members "block and tackle." On the other hand, it is hard to imagine an effective group in which members care absolutely nothing about how others value them, whether they influence the outcomes of the group's work, or whether they demonstrate leadership abilities. The leader should expect members to enter the group with rather strong but mixed feelings about competition, which they may not completely understand and are difficult to deal with openly.

Structure and Order

A set of cultural values that are related to those of rationality have to do with an emphasis on well-controlled procedures and avoidance of ambiguity and uncertainty. If a group is engaged in a hot discussion, the leader may worry about the possibility of things getting out of control, may circulate detailed agendas, implement *Robert's Rules of Order* and in other ways keep the interaction from diverging from the intended path. It is felt by many leaders to be a loss of face or a detraction from their competence if there are overt conflicts, if the agenda isn't covered, or if members won't follow the ground rules. (Consider the phrase "You are out of order.") A good leader is one who is well-organized. Some members, likewise, feel uncomfortable if things seem unstructured. They usually express strong preferences, if given an opportunity, for clear definitions of the task to be accomplished, the time framework, criteria for evaluation and operating procedures. In meetings, members usually abhor periods of silence and move quickly to try to replace ambiguity with structure. In operating work units, employees often create informal ground rules of their own when it is necessary to cope with the tensions created by uncertainty.

The point is not whether order and structure are right or wrong. Rather, it is that there are strong, culturally influenced values which say that order and structure are desirable and useful. A majority of members will likely come into the group holding such views. If a leader is one who has high standards for order and control, he/she is likely to have such a stance reinforced by the members. Leaders who have lower control needs and operate with less structure than members are used to can expect this to be a source of uneasiness.

Like most broad cultural value positions, degree of order is a two-edged sword. In many situations well-planned agendas, clearly defined tasks, and logical structures are highly useful. However, slavish adherence to *Robert's Rules of Order* in inappropriate situations (a point to be discussed later under the topic of meetings), premature agreement to procedures just to avoid ambiguity, or an obsession to keep things under control can be highly damaging to effectiveness. Before deciding on a strategy regarding degree of control and structure the leader is well advised to sort out his or her own biases, those of the members, and the realities of the situation.

Authority, Democracy, and the Sharing of Power

Any group situation poses problems of control and authority: What leadership style should be used? How much participation in the decision making shall members have? How are policies established? Until fairly recently most employees in Western countries held a set of values that said that democracy pertains to government and that on-the-job authority should be respected and obeyed. As virtually all managers know, these values are changing. It can be safely assumed, however, that in any group there will be some members who hold strong beliefs about response to authority, and that these beliefs derive from general feelings and are not specific to the group.

Often some members (but not always the older members) arrive with a cultural script to respond positively to leadership and authority. They tend to expect to be given instruction, perhaps to advise the leader but not to share in the decision making, nor to raise objections or question the leader's stance. Other members from different subcultural backgrounds do not agree with the legitimacy of imposed authority. They expect to participate rather fully in democratic decision-making processes and assume the right to question or challenge the leader. Clashes may result between the leader and members or among subgroups of members, with each side asserting the "rightness" of its stance. As is the case with most cultural value issues, the question of who is right is next to impossible to resolve because it is based on philosophical conceptions of what "ought" to be. For this discussion it is sufficient to conclude that the leader should realistically expect that members will arrive with some rather definite perceptions about appropriate responses to authority, and that these perceptions are not totally rational. That is, they are derived from cultural scripts rather than the realities of the present situation. In making a determination about how much power to share, the leader must consider the wishes of the members along with his or her own views of effective leadership, a point to be taken up in a later section on decision making.

It should be added that general cultural values are not the only source of an individual's feelings about authority. Based on experiences with authorities in our own lives, each of us develops a personalized response to authority figures. Some of us, for example, are *dependent*; we feel most comfortable relying on and following those we perceive as authorities. Others are *counter-dependent*; we tend to feel negatively toward those in authority and to resist their direction and control. Most of us fall somewhere in between the two extremes. Individual differences in personality characteristics are often not easy to sort out from culturally derived attitudes.

In-Group/Out-Group, Ethnocentrism, and Prejudice

Most of us tend to trust and feel most comfortable with other people who are like us and who belong to the same groups we do. We are suspicious and afraid of those who are different from us. These characteristics, while not particularly admirable, are probably true of most cultures, past and present.

Within groups, concerns and problems often arise in relation to differences: old with young, engineers with salesmen, black with white, talkative with quiet, new employees with old-timers, risk taking with conservative, men with women, home office with field office, etc. These difficulties arise because members bring with them values, attitudes, and feelings derived from their experience in their culture. Thus, groups deal with members' historical issues. We are taught to trust our own kind and to be wary of people who are unlike us and whom we don't understand. This attitude is, of course, prejudice. One eminent psychologist defines prejudice as "being down on something you're not up on."[1]

There is danger that those members who are alike (in terms of cultural background, vocations, or tenure in the group, for example) will form a clique (called the "in-group" if they are the majority) and discriminate in one way or another against the "out-group." This phenomenon is always troublesome, but particularly so when one of the purposes of the group is to pool the variety of different viewpoints or competencies. The human tendency to suppose that the way I and the people like me view the world is much more accurate than the way you and others like you view it is called ethnocentrism. It is the cause of a great many splits within groups and misunderstanding among different groups in the same organization or society.

Other Value Orientations

The cultural factors mentioned above comprise only a partial list. Others useful to note include:

- *The need to be seen as working hard.* Effort is important. Do something to keep busy and look busy; idleness is undesirable. Stick with the task.

- *Newness and change are positive.* A new idea gets attention. Change is likely to be seen as improvement. Old approaches cannot be best. Change may be resisted if it is threatening, but the resistance is often covert since it is unfashionable.

- *Conflict in groups is undesirable and connotes irrationality and immaturity.* It is better to suppress it or rule it out of order than to give it legitimacy by recognizing and discussing it.

• *Independence versus conformity*. Do I stand alone and follow my own path or bend to fit into the group? How can I be both a rugged individualist and a team player?

SUBCULTURES AND THEIR VALUES

Just as there are some general value orientations that are likely to show up in groups, there are also categories of people who hold sets of more or less unique values. The leader is well advised to be on the lookout for value characteristics in new groups. Most organizational consultants and trainers have learned well the lesson that unknowingly violating the norms and values of an unfamiliar group is a sure formula for failure. Similarly, the leader who shows insensitivity to the important values of a significant subgroup will build resentment. For the group leader, identification of significant subcultural groups and gaining understanding of their unique values are important steps. The danger, of course, is that by mentally placing an individual in a subcultural group we may stereotype the individual by assuming he or she has a set of characteristics we believe the group holds. ("All military officers are authoritarian. Harry is an officer, therefore he will be authoritarian.") The key is make sure our own biases don't prevent clear perception.

Male–Female Differences

Out of the current study of women's roles in organizations has come an understanding that in most societies, men and women have traditionally been socialized differently with regard to work values. That is, when they are young they are taught, often not consciously or purposefully, to adhere to different roles, values, ways of viewing themselves, and strategies for fulfilling their needs. These differences display themselves most prominently in social situations such as groups. In general (and there are obviously many exceptions) men have been socialized to wish to be seen as strong, brave, competitive, unemotional, and power-seeking.[2] Jourard observes that men are also likely to rate low in degree of self-disclosure, to hide their true feelings and concerns.[3] They tend to believe that being "manly" requires maintaining an outward appearance of calm and control, regardless of what is happening inside. Thus, there is more storing up of emotional pressures such as anger, frustration, and fear. (This is one of the reasons men suffer more stress-related illnesses.)

Men are taught not to be dependent on interpersonal relationships, to rank task goals above personal needs, and to be rational. They are told to be independent, but also to be good team players—one of the conflicts in the male role.

Women, on the other hand, have been socialized somewhat differently, although, again, it is obviously imprecise to generalize about all women. There has been a significant tendency for women to be seen as more emotional and more expressive of emotions, less overtly competitive and more dependent. They often see themselves as less powerful, and though they seek power, they may do so through less overt means than do men.

Many women have not incorporated the values of teamwork or acquired the skills for its effective performance. Also, they are less likely than men to sacrifice personal needs for group goals and may be more likely to hold relationships with others in higher priority than task performance. Women are less likely to feel positive about themselves as leaders and about their chances of success.[4]

In regard to these male–female differences, it has been pointed out that the male stereotype corresponds much more closely to the traditional concept of a leader than does the female stereotype. Clearly, women are sometimes denied leadership positions because it is assumed that aggressiveness, overt power orientation, and emotional control are essential qualifications. (Since, as we will see later, successful leadership qualities vary from one situation to another, to apply such an assumption is risky.) In the same vein, men may avoid more supportive, warm, and personally oriented behaviors under the assumption that such styles are "soft" and ineffective—again a shaky assumption without knowing the situation.

Male–female differences in socialization may raise group issues that require attention and resolution. I have never worked over an extended period of time with a group of men and women when the issue of sex differences did not arise, usually from several different facets. Sometimes the issue of sexuality comes up in regard to feelings of attraction, competition, or jealousy. More often, however, the problems have to do with stereotypes about sex role differences in style of interacting, or expectations. Usually no one says, "I believe we have a problem with male–female stereotyping in this group,"

But in a variety of ways long-held feelings and expectations about members of the opposite sex intrude into the group's activity.

Historically, insofar as organizational situations are concerned, males have tended to assume that they (the in-group) have a more valid and effective set of behaviors in relation to work. Women in the past have frequently agreed with the males and devalued their own orientation. This situation is now changing. As women gain experience in leadership roles and greater self-understanding they are less likely to devalue themselves and their different but useful styles and sensitivities. Many men, on the other hand, are becoming aware of the high physical and emotional costs of over control and nonexpression of feelings.

Other Differences

The possible subcultural differences which may appear in a group are almost too numerous to attempt to list. In addition to male–female differences, the leader may encounter:

Racial and ethnic subculture members, who bring to the group their own values about work standards, social issues, religious principles, or family matters;

Younger workers, who bring their shared values about work, dress, authority, and environmental issues;

Individuals from different socioeconomic classes who see things from a blue-collar or a white-collar perspective.

Many other differences, including but not limited to educational level, geographical background (North/South, rural/urban), and professionals in contrast to lay persons.

As I've indicated before, human beings are not comfortable with differences. Differences as basic as the ones discussed above are likely to cause trouble in the group, either in overt disagreements or more subtle conflicts. Clearly it is not possible to wash away these differences by telling members not to feel and believe as they do. Often it is useful to acknowledge that the differences do exist, discuss ways they are impacting on the group's work, and seek strategies for progressing that respect the differences but minimize their negative effect. For example, a city council found itself unable to communicate and make decisions. Part of the problem lay in basic differences of political philosophy and constituency. The members realized that all of them were developing unfavorable images because of the council's poor performance. They learned to separate the purely political matters, about which they necessarily must disagree, from the many other city problems that require only good communication and clear thinking to resolve, and to work together on those.

VALUE CONFLICTS

An individual group member sometimes finds himself or herself holding two sets of values that conflict with each other. A member may believe strongly in democratic and participative principles but be in internal conflict because the group is not choosing to go in the direction he or she prefers. Another may be torn between the need to work overtime to support the group's efforts to succeed and the responsibilities he feels to his children at home. Still another may strongly disagree with the decision a group has made but feel great pressure to support the decision because it was "made by the group."

Severe value conflicts can detract from members' ability to participate fully and freely. Although the leader cannot be responsible for resolving members' internal conflicts, it may be possible to find ways of helping to ease the pressure. It is often useful to acknowledge that value conflicts affect almost everyone and to encourage discussion of conflicts and the feelings they are causing. For example, a leader who is asking a group to go outside the office to a team-building retreat might acknowledge the pressure on members resulting from their being away from their jobs for several days and encourage discussion of ways of easing the pressure.

CHANGING VALUES IN WORK

The challenge to the leader to understand and cope with members' values is heightened by the fact that such values are, in most contemporary societies, in a continual state of change. The leader who assumes that values are, or should be, the same as they were when he or she was a new group member may encounter difficulty.

The question of whether certain values are universal, fixed, or inviolate is one of the perennial problems of human civilization. The religious answer is that some values are given to us by powers outside our world or by inspired humans codifying the wisdom of the ages and are thus unchanging. The social scientist might suggest that values grow up to protect or enhance the well-being of society or elements of it. In my view, at least in the workplace, values change because the world changes and because people find the old values put them in an unsatisfactory position for meeting their needs.

Over a decade ago Tannenbaum and Davis, an academic and an industrial leader, set down a number of value shifts they perceived beginning to occur in industrial and governmental organizations.[5] Several of these pertain to group situations. You are invited to see whether these value changes fit your own experience.

Values are seen as shifting:

"Away from resisting and fearing individual differences toward accepting utilizing them." Some organizations may be learning how to capitalize on individual differences in training, experience, point of view, and mode of operating and may utilize such differences for positive gain rather than seeing them as obstacles.

"Away from utilizing an individual primarily with reference to his job description toward viewing him as a whole person." The group setting may provide an opportunity to broaden the specialist's base of contribution to the group and provide an opportunity to develop new capabilities.

"Away from walling-off the expression of feelings toward making possible both appropriate expression and effective use of feelings." Dealing effectively with the emotional aspects of work situations means that energy formerly devoted to the repression of feelings can now be utilized for productive work, and that the underlying causes of problems can be dealt with in ways that allow them to stay solved.

"Away from marksmanship and game-playing toward authentic behavior." Strategizing, maneuvering, and wearing masks are deceptive modes of behavior. They are difficult to discard because they are defense mechanisms stemming from mistrust. However, authentic, non-devious behavior is more useful in building effective teamwork.

"Away from a primary emphasis on competition toward a much greater emphasis on collaboration." Competition sets individuals and groups against each other and creates winners and losers—often a costly style in groups and organizations with high levels of interdependency.

"Away from process work being considered unproductive effort toward seeing it as essential to effective task accomplishment." "Process work" refers to dealing with interpersonal and group dynamics that affect task accomplishment. It is the subject of the next chapter.

In the 1980s it has become popular to study changing values in work and speculate about their long-term impact. A number of popular books have raised significant issues about the way we relate to our work.[6] Basically, most observers expect greater "humanization" of work, less reliance on authority, more emphasis on participation and consensual decision making, and decentralization into smaller, more autonomous work units. Pollster Daniel Yankelovitch has paid particular attention to changing values about work.[7] He foresees higher expectations on the part of workers and a willingness to be committed to extra effort only when a "fair" return is offered in terms of rewards, both intrinsic and extrinsic. Implications for group leaders are significant. Greater amounts of work are likely to be done in decentralized, collaborative small group settings, and members will expect their work to be more interesting and to have more influence over what goes on.

SUMMARY

Individuals bring with them into groups a variety of views of the world and attitudes about the way things should be done. Some of these are individual personality characteristics as described in Chapter 2—needs, perceptions, and so on stemming from their unique psychological development. Others represent broader cultural teaching and are likely to define similarities among group members (or among subgroups within the larger group). The leader must take both factors into account in any effort to understand and deal with the dynamics of an operating group.

LEARNING AIDS

1. Your own values
    Look over the following list of major value issues in groups and indicate your own personal response to each. How would you rate yourself?

1	2	3	4	5
High rationality Low emotionality		Equal balance		Low rationality High emotionality

1	2	3	4	5
Highly competitive		Mixed		Highly collaborative

1	2	3	4	5
Highly structured Need order		Moderate		Low structure Avoid order

1	2	3	4	5
Highly authoritarian		Elements of both		Highly democratic

1	2	3	4	5
Ethnocentric (see my groups as always best/right)		Some of each		Open to other groups' values and ideas.

1	2	3	4	5
High value on hard work		Combination		Balance work with other activities

1	2	3	4	5
Positive, receptive response to change and newness		Mixed		Resist change and newness

	1	2	3	4	5

Tend to avoid conflict

Deal with conflict when necessary

Seek conflict

	1	2	3	4	5

Independence

Elements of both

Conformity

2. Think about the groups in which you are a member or leader (those identified in Chapter 1). Identify the significant *subgroups* in each insofar as significant *value differences* are concerned.

Group I _____

Group II _____

Group III _____

Group IV _____

Group V _____

Group VI _____

Group VII _____

Group VIII _____

3. Which groups that you lead contain both men and women? Are there cases of sex role stereotyping that occur?

_____

_____

_____

_____

4. What *changing values* can you identify that are causing concerns in the following areas of your life?

Group(s) you lead _____

_____

Your overall organization _____

_____

Your family or living situation _____

_____

NOTES

1. Gordon Allport, interview with Richard Evans, *American Psychological Association Monitor* 14 (1983): 39.

2. Robert A. Fein, "Examining the Nature of Masculinity" in *Beyond Sex Roles*, Alice G. Sargent, ed. (St. Paul, MN: West Publishing Company, 1977).

3. Sidney M. Jourard, "Some Lethal Aspects of the Male Role," in *The Transparent Self* (Princeton, NJ: Van Nostrand, 1964), pp. 46–55.

4. Several readings in Sargent, *Beyond Sex Roles*. See, for example, Elizabeth Aries, "Male–Female Interpersonal Styles in All Male, All Female and Mixed Groups," pp. 292–301.

5. Robert Tannenbaum and Sheldon A. Davis, "Values, Man and Organizations," *Industrial Management Review* 10 (1969): 67–83.

6. See, for example, Marilyn Ferguson, *The Aquarian Conspiracy*, (Los Angeles: J. P. Tarcher, 1980).

7. Daniel Yankelovich, *New Rules: Searching for Self-Fulfillment in a World Turned Upside Down* (New York: Random House, 1981).

4

BASIC GROUP DYNAMICS:
UNDERSTANDING
HOW GROUPS WORK

The members of the computer programming department were highly trained technicians. When working individually they had the capacity to solve most problems they faced. When working together in project teams, however, their technical potential seemed to be buried beneath squabbles. They splintered into cliques that argued about how things should be done; they communicated so poorly that important information often got lost; and there seemed to be very little focus on overall project and department goals. Mary Hutchins, supervisor of the unit, was at her wit's end. Trained to analyze situations, to dissect them into their important components, she set out to diagnose her group. But what factors should she look for? What are the variables involved in poor teamwork? What models could she use to understand what was happening in her unit?

Now that we have identified the characteristics that members bring into the group with them, we can move to an analysis of the internal workings of groups. Groups, as we have said, have been analyzed and described from a variety of points of view, and a growing list of group interaction variables has emerged. Yet there is no simple scheme for studying groups that provides more than a narrow viewpoint of limited use. Groups, by their nature, are complex. Our challenge is to develop a concise description of group dynamics that provides adequate information for practical application to work situations.

Psychologists interested in complex learning have described the value of developing a *cognitive map*. By this they mean a clear overview in the "mind's eye" of the phenomenon under study and a set of categories or concepts that help bring order to a complicated situation. Our intention is to help the reader build a cognitive map of groups that he or she can use in actual situations. The map will be drawn to medium scale. No attempt will be made to cover all details or to summarize the myriad findings about groups. Such facets can be the subject of further study, if desired. On the other hand, the map will define the territory in more detail than the standard management texts, which too often limit themselves to demonstrating that two-way communication is better than one-way, and that democratic leadership is better than autocratic under certain circumstances.

We will begin our analysis with an overall framework and a set of four basic dimensions of group activity. We will then explore the important distinction between content and process and discuss some of the major process issues that confront groups. The next topic will be those intriguing aspects of groups that exist beneath the surface of the obvious. This will be followed by a discussion of why members choose to join and participate in groups, and the chapter will conclude with a look at some of the major types of roles played by group members as they attempt to help the group cope with its tasks and maintenance.

GROUPS AS SOCIAL SYSTEMS

When we begin the study of groups it is useful to have available an overall conceptual scheme to use in our thinking. Several have been proposed.[1] We will begin by viewing the group as a social system. A group social system denotes an entity in which there is: (a) a continuous series of actions and interactions (members say or do something and thereby elicit a response from other members); (b) interdependence (success depends on members meshing their efforts); (c) the group must strive to maintain stability or equilibrium in its internal functioning; (d) there is some degree of structure (members play different roles, specialize, and establish hierarchies); (3) communication among members and with other systems is required for effective operation; and (f) the group has a boundary or separation from other systems. Thus, the study of groups requires tuning in on an ongoing interactive system and attempting to understand its dynamics.

A next step in developing a usable map of group dynamics components involves identifying the major functions of the social system. At a general level, what functions do groups perform? Many of the activities and interactions can be classified into one or more of a set of four basic functions. These categories provide the group leader a beginning reference point for assessing a group.

• Adapting to the requirements and pressures of the external environment.

• Performing activities instrumental to accomplishment of the task.

• The expression and management of feelings.

• Integration of members into a cohesive and cooperative system.

Adapting to the Requirements and Pressures of the External Environment

No group, least of all a working group in a complex organization, exists in a vacuum. Groups are often created initially by the larger organization to which they belong. Their operating processes, salary plans, and personnel policies are established or heavily influenced by this environment. And the ultimate success of the group is usually evaluated by that external environment according to standards it establishes.

Some groups may, for a while, attempt to function as though they are relatively free from the environment. The design unit may merrily crank out new ideas and plans with little regard for the ability of the manufacturing department to produce the gadgets or the sales department to market them. Or a university department may develop its course offerings according to the professional interests and conveniences of the faculty to the neglect of the wishes of the students, the funding body, or the university administration. Sooner or later, however, in any but a fantasy world, the group will be held responsible to the context within which it operates.

For most groups a certain proportion of the time and energy goes to coping with the environment. Questions such as, "What resources do we have to work with? What does the larger organization expect of us? How do we interpret our directives? How will our performance be evaluated?" are questions that deal with the relationship between the group and its environment. It should also be mentioned that a group may either consciously or unconsciously use the environment as a scapegoat for avoiding responsibility for its own failures. Spending inordinate amounts of time damning other groups with statements such as, "We can't do anything without more support from the people at the top," may be examples of such avoidance.

Another aspect of the group's need to cope with the environment has already been discussed. That is the imposition of values from the environment and culture on the group's operation. We discussed, for example, the impact on the group of an environment that strongly values competition.

Performing Activities Instrumental to Accomplishment of the Task

For all groups except those whose purpose is purely social, the task (or mission or goal) provides the primary reason for existence. And in well-functioning working groups the majority of time and energy (though by no means all) are spent performing those activities that are instrumental to accomplishing the task. In discussion-type working groups such as committees, task activities include generating and sharing pertinent information, setting priorities, problem solving and/or decision making, and evaluating actual or anticipated consequences of various actions. In groups whose task involves physical labor as well as talk, performance includes both the skill and efficiency of the labor along with such mental functions as planning, resource allocation, and quality control.

The function of the working group is to transform the time, energy, knowledge, and skill of its members into tangible or intangible outcomes. This task-oriented side of a group's life poses issues to be dealt with: Do we have the necessary skills, information, and technology? What resources are required? Are guidelines and procedures clear and usable? How do we place the right person in the right role? How can we best organize this group in terms of structure and function?

The Expression and Management of Feelings

If human groups operated purely logically and rationally their problems would be limited to those of organizing for the task. Since, as we have seen, humans are at once both rational and nonrational, a sizable proportion of what happens falls into the domain of social–emotional issues. The fact that emotions are stirred up as members interact and these emotions influence the way people work on the task means that a part of every group's challenge has to do with the expression and management of members' feelings.

In some groups, the reality of social–emotional issues is either not known or is ignored. It is assumed that members bring their rational selves to the group, operate logically and coolly, and any incidental manifestations of feeling, such as arguments or jealousies, are simply idiosyncrasies that are best overridden by rational control or ignored. This logic might work in a short-term meeting situation, but is fraught with risk in longer-term operations. Strong and persistent feelings that are not recognized and dealt with are highly likely to manifest themselves in one way or another in the group's work.

The manifestation of feelings in groups may occur in a variety of ways and levels, and there are many techniques for their management. In addition to the avoidance approach, some groups use a highly controlled strategy, such as *Robert's Rules of Order*. In this technique member interactions are channelled into a prescribed format so that limits are placed on the amount and kind of expression allowed. Still other groups expect and tolerate a certain amount of emotionality in the form of arguments, "getting things off their chests," or—on the more positive side—expressions of praise and support. Still fewer groups take time to decide how they want to handle the expression and management of feelings and to develop norms and strategies to support their decision.

Integration of Members into a Cohesive and Cooperative System

Highly significant factors in any ongoing group are the members' sense of "groupness"—their desire and ability to function together as a unit. Members of a new group, after pulling together and weathering their first crisis, are likely to exclaim, "We have become a team!" The spirit of an athletic team and the pride and solidarity of a group working toward an important and inspiring cause are other examples. These are the ingredients that distinguish a cohesive group from a collection of people or a mob.

Integration depends in part on members' feelings. But it also relies on appropriate behaviors and mechanisms. A football team in which everyone tries to play quarterback and no one knows how to work together would fall apart, no matter how high the spirit. Clearly, a work unit in which no one has pride or confidence will experience minimal success. But so will one where pride is high but members have not worked out the roles, mechanisms, and mutual responsibilities necessary for collaboration. From this perspective, the aspect of group integration is the one in which the concept of system is most clearly applicable.

Not only do the four dimensions describe the major aspects of a group's activities, they also provide a framework for assessing group performance. A leader who wishes to monitor the group's development can gain a fairly complete picture by considering the outcome aspects of the dimensions:

• *Adaptation to the external environment.* The ultimate and long-range assessment of a group's effectiveness is often conducted by an outside agent, such as upper management. Has the group carried its share of the load? Has it lived up to expectations? Does it have effective relations with other interdependent systems? Has it developed a healthy enough relationship to its environment to survive over time?

• *Task performance.* Is the group accomplishing the assignment set out for it within appropriate time and efficiency limits? Are the goals or missions or products or services being attained according to available measures of performance?

• *Social–emotional state.* Are members' feelings about the task, the group, each other, and themselves positive and facilitative, or negative and detrimental? Is the group able to recognize and deal with emotional issues that arise or do feelings stymie progress by being swept under the rug, to fester and eat away at group morale?

• *Integration and collaboration.* Is the group a cohesive and well-organized system that develops the norms and mechanisms needed to function smoothly, or is it a fractionated and uncoordinated collection of people? Do members' skills, interests, and information combine to provide a synergistic process or does the mixture hamper cooperation and minimize output?

CONTENT AND PROCESS

When we observe a group in operation we are aware of an obvious series of things happening at the *manifest* level. That is, there are interactions occurring among members that are public, direct, and equally observable by all. People talk with each other, some more than others. The speed and volume of the discussion changes, as does the subject matter. Sometimes there is an observable outcome; a decision is made, a problem is solved, and a project completed. Members may come and go, and the group may divide into two or more subunits.

At this out in the open, manifest level the most obvious aspect of what is happening (and the one that we usually pay most attention to) is the *content*—the subject matter or topic under discussion. The content may be a delay on the production line, a problem employee, a new employment opportunities program, or last night's bowling tournament. Often, though not always, the content pertains to the group's reason for existence, the substance of the work it has been put together to do. When asked to observe a group and comment on its functioning, students new to the field often focus at this manifest content level (as they do in ordinary meetings). They observe that some members seem not to have much information about the subject, the group often gets away from the topic, very little new light is shed after the first half hour, and that the group failed to consider some important points. That, however, is only part of the story.

As people continue to observe and analyze group behavior, they usually become increasingly aware that there is a good deal happening that goes beyond the obvious flow of information about the content. In fact, there is a continuous chain of events that pertains to *how* the group is dealing with the content. These events and the interactions and feelings that accompany them, are referred to as the group's *process*. The process is the latent level in the group's life. It encompasses those aspects of the group's operation that cannot be observed directly, but must be inferred from watching behavioral patterns that unfold and making sense out of them by interpreting them through the use of a theory or concept. The need to infer what is going on at the latent or process level in a group is the major requirement faced by the student of groups. The thoughts and feelings of members and their subtle interaction process can never be fully understood, but educated guesses can be made and then tested out in subsequent observations and actions. Because of this, group leadership remains part science and part art.

The content/process distinction is one of the most basic and useful tools in the field. It will be used throughout the remainder of this book, and later sections will discuss techniques for dealing with some of the more significant process issues that may arise. A group's ability to perform effectively at the process level will have a significant impact on its ability to deal successfully with its content, (i.e., to accomplish its task). A leader's ability to diagnose problems at the process level and intervene to help the group understand and resolve those problems is one measure of his or her effectiveness. The leader who can direct and/or participate in the group's content discussion while at the same time being aware of and dealing with process has mastered the elements of competence.

Some of the major categories of process elements in a group's operation include the following:

• *Communication.* The degree to which information flow is accurate, open and honest, and evenly distributed.

• *Cooperation versus competition.* The degree to which members work toward common goals as opposed to engaging in win/lose behaviors.

• *Control issues.* Struggles and feelings related to who plays leadership roles, styles of management, degree to which control is shared, power struggles.

• *Commitment.* Degree of agreement between individual needs and group goals; members' allegiance to the group and its purposes.

• *Conformity.* Degree to which norms and pressures reduce individuality and demand adherence to group standards.

• *Conflict.* Ways in which the group deals with or avoids its differences, rivalries, and animosities.

- *Cohesiveness/comradeship.* Group members' feelings for each other and for the group and their interest in keeping the group together.

- *Confidence/trust.* Willingness to risk possible ridicule, attack, or manipulation by entrusting one's true feelings, ideas, and experimental behavior to other members.

- *Intimacy.* Degree to which group members develop close, warm interpersonal relationships in contrast to formal, distant, and cool relations.

- *Competence.* Degree to which members are perceived by themselves and others as having or not having the abilities and knowledge required to carry their share of the work.

- *Change.* Ability of the group to adapt and modify or redirect its behavior in order to meet new demands or respond to changed conditions.

- *Climate.* The emotional tone of the group that impacts members (defensive versus supportive, friendly versus hostile, tense versus relaxed, etc.).

It is helpful for the leader to realize that any one or more of this list of a dozen process issues may arise in a group at any point and thus affect the group's work. These factors represent the most basic dilemmas in human interaction and vividly illustrate that groups are microcosms of the society in which they exist. If a group is floundering—failing at its task and/or losing its cohesiveness—it is common to blame lack of information (content), insufficient time, or elusiveness of the ideal solution. Yet more often than is realized, one or more process dilemmas are the cause. For example, unresolved control issues may be bothering members—unclear leadership patterns, rivalries for domination, or fears of being seen as too pushy. Members may or may not be consciously aware of their feelings, but so long as they remain unresolved the group will continue to expend emotional energy on its process problems and be hampered in its ability to do the job. (These 12 issues will be discussed in greater detail in Chapter 6.)

Content as a Clue to Process

Up to this point we have been talking as if content and process are entirely separate phenomena. Actually they are not. While it is helpful to make a clear distinction between them for purposes of understanding, they are, of course, simply different facets of a group's operation and thus are related. Leaders and group facilitators find, in fact, that themes in the content of a discussion are often a good clue to underlying process concerns. Some such linkages are obvious. If what one member says bears little relationship to what was said before him, and if this behavior continues like a circle of TV sets all tuned to different channels, there is a communication problem that involves lack of listening. (It may also, of course, involve other related process issues, such as high levels of competition, especially if members are cutting each other off before being allowed to finish a statement.) Other content indicators of process issues may be a good deal more subtle and may take more time and effort to tease out. Discussions that seem to stay at very "safe" superficial levels without ever dealing with important or strong ideas or feelings may indicate that the trust level is low and members are afraid to risk personal disclosure. Or if the discussion continually wanders off the topic and progress seems slow, members may feel low commitment due to lack of interest in the goal.[2]

A good rule of thumb is as follows: if group members are competent with the content (if they have the necessary information and skill), if the physical circumstances seem adequate (members are not overcome with fatigue, smoke, etc.), and the goals and purposes are clearly understood, poor performance and/or low morale are likely to be due to process issues within the group.

It must be emphasized that a group is not likely to be helped by the leader who admonishes, "This group is doing so poorly that there must be a process problem! Come on, what is it?" It may be possible for the leader, once a supportive climate has been established, to say, "Something seems to be blocking our progress. I notice we're interrupting each other as if we're competing for the floor. Can we take time out from the task and talk about it?" This skill of facilitating (helping the group understand and deal with its problems rather than giving orders) is an important one, and is the subject of much of this book.

It would be convenient if there were a set of formulas for recognizing process issues from the content events occurring at the manifest level. Unfortunately, such a tidy aid is not available. There are too many possibilities and variations. However, the following rules of thumb provide a place to begin:

• Monitor the group's climate. Begin by staying in touch with your own feeling reactions. Often we pick up many subtle cues to what is happening in the group and begin to have emotional responses without clearly understanding them. If you begin to feel bored or tense or impatient, ask yourself why. There is a very good chance others are feeling the same way.

• Look for communication problems. A healthy communication climate means that members are able to speak openly and frankly about their feelings and ideas, and also listen to the ideas and feelings of others. The discussion should stay on the subject most of the time and should progress toward the goals of pooling of information, correcting errors or gaps in the data, and reaching a point where the group is ready to make a decision or take action.

• Be aware of how the group is working with the differences among its members. Is there competition, conflict, coercion, and if so, why? Are differences dealt with openly and directly or avoided?

• Look for recurrent content themes that do not seem to be moving the group toward its goals. The group may be unwittingly using them either to vent frustrations (talking about unresponsive national leaders when they are mad at their own leader) or as a vehicle for avoiding uncomfortable issues (debating the pros and cons of women as managers when there are unresolved male–female feelings in the group).

• Train yourself to attend to nonverbal information. Members communicate much about their feelings and their membership through their "body language." Do facial expressions indicate interest or boredom? Do sitting positions demonstrate tension? Are members indicating involvement by leaning toward the center of the group or detachment by leaning away?

Once a process issue has been identified, the leader must decide what to do about it. Much of the rest of this book deals with understanding and resolving process issues. The solution depends on the issue, member characteristics, and the content. Misunderstandings or lack of goal clarity, for example, may be dealt with rather easily by careful discussion. Latent conflict is usually much more difficult to deal with, and may require hearing out bad feelings and patient negotiation. In any event, the leader has made the first step in problem solving when he or she identifies the process issues that are blocking group progress. Some leaders who wish to improve the productivity of groups attempt to do so solely by structure and control (rules, procedures, assignments, etc.). To utilize only this approach ignores the realities of the social–emotional system and risks damaging morale, commitment, and cohesiveness.

PHASES IN GROUP DEVELOPMENT

Groups, like individuals, are not static. They develop and change over time. The process issues faced by a new group are usually somewhat different from those of an older one. If a group resolves the issues that confront it (or if it is lucky enough not to be bothered by serious problems), it stands a good chance of moving successfully through its phases of development to become mature, healthy, and well integrated. It is useful for the leader to know at what stage the group is working and thus what are the issues with which it is likely to grapple. The following phases are a composite from the writings of several observers.[3] They often, but not always, occur in the order shown.

1. The first process issues to arise after a new group comes together often have to do with membership and acceptance. This is frequently a time of feelings of threat and concern for identity. People wonder, "Who am I in this group? How will I be viewed by others? How will my contributions stack up? Will I be accepted and supported by these other people?" This phase can be moved through for most members when a climate of mutual trust begins to develop. The leader can assist by openly acknowledging and accepting the underlying feelings ("It's not uncommon for members of a new group to feel a little apprehensive about what will be expected of them.") and by encouraging an acquaintance process ("Let's set aside some time at this point to get better acquainted with each other and find out why we're here.").

2. The next stage is likely to have to do with the balancing of individual and group goals and needs. The group usually begins with some official statement of purpose which may or may not coincide with its real function. Members arrive with a more or less clear picture of the official purpose, and with their own set of needs and expectations. One significant issue is whether members will accept and "own" the group goals as compatible with their own goals, or whether they will begin to attempt to bend or subvert the group goals to their own ends. Another issue is whether the goals and needs of the various members are compatible or whether effort will be spent contesting goals and directions.

It is well for the leader to be on the lookout for that stage in the developmental process where group and individual goals are being clarified, tested, and negotiated. If a clear understanding and ownership of group goals is not reached and if reasonable integration of individual needs is not attained, the unresolved issues are highly likely to cause trouble later on.

3. Communication and decision-making processes often assume importance after a group has identified its tasks and begins to seek productivity. At this stage questions need to be formulated, information must be generated, ideas tested, alternatives identified, and ways of deciding on action agreed to. Task-oriented behaviors often predominate. Issues have to do with whether people communicate effectively, whether they are willing to listen to each other, whether the data flow is open and spontaneous or constricted, and whether enough internal control develops to keep the discussion on the topic.

An important element in the group's development at this point is whether the communication process evolves in such a way as to promote positive relationships among members. The preponderance of research indicates that in groups in which members are able to express their feelings as well as their ideas openly with minimal fear of risk or ridicule a healthier climate evolves—that is, the communication process is more supportive of morale and effectiveness.

The effective leader could do worse than to see herself or himself as guardian of the communication process. Are members speaking straightforwardly and openly without undue guardedness and jockeying? Are they listening to and responding to each other? Does the climate seem to be supportive of creativity and reasonable risk taking as opposed to self-defense?

4. As the group works together on the task, issues of control and organization almost invariably arise. Members see things differently, have different needs, engage in competition, and get into conflicts. Some means has to be found to resolve differences and keep members coordinated and pulling in the same general direction at least part of the time. One aspect of control has to do with leadership. Is leadership vested in one person or is it shared? Is the style democratic or authoritarian? Other aspects include degree and kind of structure, task assignments, work schedules, and output measures. Member's reactions to the leadership and control systems are crucial. Do they accept and adhere to the controls or do they rankle against them, avoid them when possible, and always strive to change them? The wise leader realizes that if they are to function effectively over time, leadership control mechanisms must be accepted by the members. In the next chapter we will discuss in detail some of the characteristics and practices of effective group leadership.

These four developmental phases describe fairly well, at a general level, the particular sets of issues faced by groups as they evolve. It is not necessarily an exclusive list. For example, some groups pass through other kinds of phases, such as the problem of how close and personal to be with each other. Other groups may not experience all the phases, or may experience them in a different order. Nevertheless, the list can be helpful in forewarning the leader and members about some of the process problems they are likely to have to face.

DYNAMICS BENEATH THE SURFACE

Because group participation may significantly impact on those psychological needs of members that we discussed in Chapter 2 (self-image, self-respect, belonging, status, etc.) members often feel a certain amount of risk and tension. They may, consciously or unconsciously, perceive a group situation as one in which there is a possibility of being ridiculed or devalued (seen as incompetent, weak, or bad). This is especially true for people who have had negative experiences in groups in the past, such as being embarrassed by a teacher in front of the class, making painful mistakes in a piano recital, showing up inappropriately dressed at a party and being teased, or being made a scapegoat in a family conflict.

For these reasons a good deal of incongruent behavior often characterizes groups. By incongruence we refer to outward behavior that does not correspond to the underlying feelings and attitudes held by the person. Members, in order to protect themselves, often keep their process concerns under the table. They assume that sharing their fears, confusions, and incapabilities would be costly. This tendency has led one observer, Will Schutz, to label this aspect of groups the *interpersonal underworld.*[4]

FIGURE 4.1 THE JOHARI WINDOW[5]

	Known to Self	Not Known to Self
Known to Others	I Area of Free Activity	II Blind Area
Not Known to Others	III Avoided or Hidden Area	IV Area of Unknown Activity

Several useful ideas have been developed to assist in understanding incongruence. One graphic approach has been dubbed the "JOHARI window" after its originators, Joe Luft and Harry Ingham.[6] In the "window" or matrix shown below, the vertical columns represent the areas of information that are either known or not known to the "self"—the individual group member in question. The rows represent the areas of information that are either known or not known to the other members of the same group. The point of the diagram is to illustrate that there are some things about each member that are known to both him/herself and the other group members (the "area of free activity"). This may include general descriptive information (name, rank, and serial number), physical attributes, and information about ideas and feelings that the individual has chosen to share with others.

The *blind area* encompasses information the other members have about the individual in question, but that the individual himself does not have. This could include how the individual impacts on others, mannerisms he/she may not be aware of, areas of misinformation or erroneous judgment, or where, unknown to the individual, inner feelings are being revealed by nonverbal cues.

The *hidden area* covers information that the individual has chosen not to reveal to others. This may include not only skeletons in the closet and personal and private facts, but also positive or negative feelings about the group, data pertinent to the task, and hidden agendas, which will be discussed in the next section.

The *unknown area* includes processes that are out of the awareness of the individual and the group, but are nevertheless impacting on the group. These could include unconscious material, group phenomena not understood by those present, or shared lack of information.

The value of the JOHARI window is that it clearly illustrates the possibilities for incongruence in a group. At any given time, the open area of free and full communication is constricted. Each member is operating with only partial information about him/herself and about other members' ideas, feelings, and intentions. Generally speaking, the larger the area of free activity in relation to others, the more effective the group. This is because members will have more complete information to operate with and also because they have to devote less attention and energy to covering up and wearing a mask in order to maintain the incongruence between outer and inner selves.

An example of a constricted area of free activity would be a new group in which members do not know and trust each other and thus reveal very little about themselves. Since members do not understand each others' intentions, needs, views, and reactions, there is a minimum of common ground for them to work with. The atmosphere is likely to remain stiff and standoffish until members risk exchanging more information so that they may come to understand each other better.

Increasing the size of the open area (as shown below) is not easy in many groups. The possibilities are for members to provide more information about their ideas and feelings, thus decreasing the size of the hidden area, and to share more of their perceptions of each other through feedback in order to decrease the blind area. Both involve risk and must be worked on gradually as members venture into new areas of communication. As the trust level rises, openness and congruence can increase. In working groups the appropriate goal is not the revelation of one's innermost secrets or basest urges, but to be more open with ideas and feelings pertinent to the business and relations at hand and devote less energy to maintaining masks. Usually little can or should be done to attempt to decrease the unknown area except in therapy groups and some training groups, which have self-exploration and deeper self-understanding as major purposes.

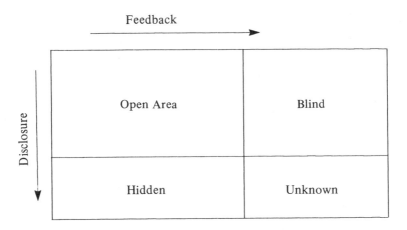

A related concept, the *hidden agenda*, describes another aspect of a group's underground—that of process issues involving unspoken but influential concerns about group goals or operations.[7] In a group there is usually a formal or at least informal agenda or set of purposes. It is usually assumed that members have accepted this agenda and are committed to working on it. It may be the case, however, that members have their own private agendas which they keep hidden but which influence behavior. One member may fear changes in traditional ways of doing things and may act subtly to block the group from reaching a decision on a new program by asking innumerable questions, stirring up conflict, and so on. Another may feel competitive with others and seek to outdo them. Still another may distrust the group, and while feigning openness withhold significant information.

Sometimes a hidden agenda may extend beyond a single individual to include a segment of the group or the entire group itself. For example, several members of a group may share a feeling of animosity toward the leader and may convertly seek to sabotage his or her influence. Or the members of a committee may have been pressured to serve even though they are not in agreement with the official goals. They may express their "lack of understanding" of the goals, suggest numerous modifications, and fail to make any substantial contribution toward the official goal—all without publicly owning up to their real agenda.

The alert leader should always expect some hidden agendas in a group setting because it is not likely that there will be perfect agreement between each individual's needs and the group's purpose. Not all hidden agendas, of course, have a negative effect. Some members, for example, may want the group to be highly successful because it enhances their visibility. However, it is safest to assume that there may be hidden agendas that may lead the group off course, and to be on the lookout for evidence of them.

Considerable sensitivity should be used in dealing with hidden agendas (as well as the obscure areas of the JOHARI window). Sometimes, but not always, "surfacing" the incongruence is helpful. Perhaps the most useful question to ask oneself is, "How threatened will members be if confronted with the hidden item?" If the threat level is too high, members may be driven into more incongruent behavior rather than being helped to deal with the issue. If the threat level is fairly low, it is often useful either to point out the hidden agenda as the leader perceives it, or to raise a question about whether there is a hidden agenda operating. If the hidden agenda can be brought into the open and dealt with successfully by the group, a major blockage in group progress can often be removed.

MEMBERSHIP AND PARTICIPATION

In Chapter 2 we discussed member motivation and developed an approach to understanding the needs individuals have that attract them to membership and participation in groups. In this section we will continue that line of thinking, but with the focus on the group and the kinds of positive or negative incentives it offers.

Whether an individual seeks membership in a group (by applying for a job or volunteering for a committee), joins as a part of regular work responsibilities, or is pressured into the situation, he or she makes a decision about how and to what degree to participate. One can participate to the hilt and be constantly involved, expending maximum energy and seeking and contributing helpful ideas. Or one can participate at a modest and responsible level, doing what is required and perhaps a little more, but not extending oneself. One can also get by with minimal effort, being present but largely unheard from, practicing that well-established body of techniques for muddling through. The choice one makes depends to a significant degree on the anticipated tradeoff or exchange between the *effort* of participation and the *rewards* of membership.

From the leader's point of view, it is crucial to remember that group members who perceive the reward/effort ratio to be unfavorable for themselves are unlikely to expend much energy and creativity. Punishment (negative reward) is, of course, one tool that can be applied in such situations. However, it is fraught with problems: particularly, (a) the amount of punishment one can legitimately use with adults in the work world is limited; (b) those individuals whom we most need to make our groups productive usually have the most alternatives elsewhere; and (c) punishment, or threat of it, may force a member to be present and to work, but it rarely can extract creativity, commitment, and morale. Thus, the leader often finds it most useful to seek ways to build positive motivation into group situations.

The concept of the *psychological contract* developed by Edgar Schein proves to be a useful tool in this regard.[8] Schein points out that when an individual enters a group or organization there are two sets of expectations established. The individual expects certain benefits in return for his or her time, energy, and talents. These may include a variety of tangible and intangible factors (pay, status, enjoyment, professional development, security, freedom to speak out, etc.). The group, on the other hand, usually expects certain things from the member. (Or, more accurately, members of the group have a more or less common set of expectations of the individual.) In return for the rewards of membership, group rules require certain services from the member (perhaps regular attendance, adherence to rules, contribution of skill, respect for the leader, etc.). These cross-expectations constitute the psychological contract. Often the contract is implicit and unspoken; neither party expresses its expectations openly to the other, but both assume there is mutual agreement. If there is a "bad" contract, that is, if the member expects things the group does not intend to provide, or vice versa, there is likely to be disaffection. The member's morale may suffer, sense of commitment may fall, and the contribution to the group's goals begin to slip.

The problem with the psychological contract is that it is usually not discussed and often even unrecognized by both sides. Thus, it is difficult to cope with issues of membership and mutual expectations when they have not been legitimized as essential considerations in a group's life. It behooves any leader to first ask himself or herself, "Just what is the nature of the psychological contract we wish members to enter into with this group? What are the group's expectations of its members, what does it propose to provide in return for members' services? What do members expect to gain from their participation?" Later it may be appropriate to raise the same questions with the members themselves.

If the member expectations are much higher than the group leader plans to provide, some action must be taken or there is a risk of losing members, either physically or psychologically. Perhaps discussion of mutual expectations will help modify the expectations of the members. Perhaps also the leader's expectations may change. Alternatively, members and the leader may find different approaches to operations that will allow more of everyone's needs and expectations to be met, thus making the group a much more viable entity in the long run.

The important point to remember is that *the psychological contract exists at all times*, either openly or covertly. If it is recognized and explored early in the group the leader does not have to trust to luck that everyone's expectations complement each other. The best strategy is a legitimate and open discussion and a renegotiation of contributions and benefits, if necessary. "Contracting" is a technique that can be of value to the leader.

ROLES OF GROUP MEMBERS

The discussion thus far in this chapter has focused largely on overall group phenomena (dimensions, processes, etc.). Another perspective that leaders and scholars have found useful has to do with the kinds of roles played by the individual group members. It turns out that although each member is unique, there are certain general kinds of roles that tend to be enacted regardless of the group or the task. These informal roles usually are not planned. In fact, members usually are not aware of them. But they may significantly help or hinder group operation. In a study of functional roles of members of training groups, Benne and Sheats classified participation into the categories of *group task roles*, *group building and maintenance roles*, and *individual roles.*[9]

Task Roles

The task of the discussion groups studied was to select, define, and solve common problems. The member roles that pertained primarily to the accomplishment of the task were:

• The initiator–contributor suggests or proposes to the group new ideas or a changed way of regarding the group problem or goal.

• The information seeker asks for clarification of suggestions made, for authoritative information and facts pertinent to the problem being discussed.

• The opinion seeker asks not primarily for the facts of the case but for a clarification of the values involved.

• The information giver offers facts or generalizations that are "authoritative" or relate his own experience to the group problem.

• The opinion giver states her belief or opinion pertinently to a suggestion made or to alternative suggestions.

• The elaborator spells out suggestions in terms of examples or developed meanings, offers a rationale for suggestions previously made, and tries to deduce how an idea or suggestion would work out if adopted by the group.

• The coordinator shows or clarifies the relationships among various ideas and suggestions, tries to pull ideas and suggestions together, or tries to coordinate the activities of various members or subgroups.

• The orienter defines the position of the group with respect to its goals by summarizing what has occurred, points to departures from agreed upon directions or goals, or raises questions about the direction that the discussion is taking.

• The evaluator–critic subjects the accomplishment of the group to some standard or set of standards of group functioning in the context of the group task.

• The energizer prods the group to action or decision, attempts to stimulate or arouse the group to greater or "higher quality" activity.

• The procedural technician expedites group movement by doing things for the group (performing routine tasks, e.g., distributing materials, rearranging the seating, running the recording machine, etc.).

• The recorder writes down suggestions, makes a record of group decisions, writes down the product of discussion, and acts as the group memory.

Group Building and Maintenance Roles

Maintenance role behaviors focus not directly on the task itself but on building and maintaining the group on those areas of expression and management of feelings and integration and collaboration that we discussed at the beginning of the chapter:

• The encourager praises, agrees with and accepts the contribution of others, and indicates warmth and solidarity toward other group members.

• The harmonizer mediates the differences between other members, attempts to reconcile disagreements, and relieves tension in conflict situations through jesting or pouring oil on the troubled waters.

• The compromiser operates from within a conflict in which his idea or position is involved. He may offer compromise by yielding status, admitting error, disciplining himself to maintain group harmony, or by meeting others half-way in moving with the group.

• The gate-keeper and expediter attempts to keep communication channels open by encouraging or facilitating the participation of others ("We haven't got the ideas of Mr. X yet.") or by proposing regulation of the flow of communication ("Why don't we limit the length of our contributions so that everyone will have a chance to contribute?").

• The standard setter or ego ideal expresses standards for the group to attempt to achieve in its functioning or applies standards in evaluating the quality of group processes.

• The group observer and commentator keeps records of various aspects of group process and feeds such data with proposed interpretations into the group's evaluation of its own procedures.

• The follower goes along with the movement of the group, more or less passively accepting the ideas of others, serving as an audience in group discussion and decision.

Individual Roles

Not all member roles are relevant to the group and its task. Some are self-oriented and have to do with individual agendas or unresolved process difficulties. Individual roles are often not helpful and sometimes they are destructive.

• The aggressor may work in many ways—deflating the status of others, expressing disapproval of the values, acts, or feelings of others, attacking the group or the problem it is working on, joking aggressively, or showing envy toward another's contribution by trying to take credit for it.

• The blocker tends to be negativistic and stubbornly resistant, disagreeing and opposing without or beyond "reason" and attempting to maintain or bring back an issue after the group has rejected or bypassed it.

• The recognition seeker works in various ways to call attention to herself, whether through boasting, reporting on personal achievements, acting in unusual ways, or struggling to prevent being placed in an "inferior" position.

• The self-confessor uses the audience opportunity that the group setting provides to express personal, non–group-oriented feeling, insight, or ideology.

• The playboy makes a display of his lack of involvement in the group's processes. This may take the form of cynicism, nonchalance, horseplay, and other more or less studied forms of "out-of-field" behavior.

• The dominator tries to assert authority or superiority in manipulating the group or certain members of the group. This domination may take the form of flattery, of asserting a superior status or right to attention, giving directions authoritatively, or interrupting the contribution of others.

• The help seeker attempts to call forth a sympathy response from other group members or from the whole group, whether through expressions of insecurity, personal confusion, or depreciation of himself.

• The special interest pleader speaks for the "small businessman," the "grass-roots community," the "housewife," "labor," etc., usually cloaking her own prejudices or biases in the stereotype that best fits one's individual need.

Any one individual may, of course, play multiple roles; and these roles may change from time to time. In fact, one characteristic of successful groups is that leaders and members are able to play a variety of helpful task and maintenance roles when conditions call for them. The researchers point out that at different stages of development a group's need for functional roles changes. For example, the role of evaluator–critic will probably be less useful early in a problem-solving process, while information is being gathered and alternatives identified, than it will later when options must be evaluated, some discarded, and a final decision reached. The trick for group members who would like to perform as effectively as possible is to learn which roles are most useful at different stages.

There are no exact formulas for measuring the correct proportions of task-oriented versus maintenance-oriented behavior. However, Shepherd reviewed the research on a similar model of member behavior, the Bales Interaction Process Analysis.[10] The average ratio of social–emotional acts to instrumental (task) acts in normal groups was two instrumental acts to each social–emotional act. A very high proportion of task acts (a ratio greater than 2:1) may mean that the group is highly task-oriented or that social–emotional acts are being avoided for various reasons. A high proportion of social–emotional acts (ratio of less than two instrumental acts to each social–emotional act) may mean avoidance of work or that social–emotional concerns require attention. Other factors such as group norms and reward systems also influence the ratios. Important concerns for the leader are whether group members have the skills to play the various roles and the sensitivity to know when to play them. A role overplayed or played at the wrong time is as problematic as a role not available when needed. One characteristic of people with poor group skills is that they have very limited repertoires of task and maintenance roles and therefore keep playing the same roles whether or not they are relevant or useful to what the group is trying to accomplish.

Some groups develop norms and expectations that encourage certain roles and discourage others. For example, a group in which commitment is low may exert subtle pressures against a member who pushes too hard on task roles; or a group that feels uncomfortable with conflict may reinforce the harmonizer. A group's selectivity about which roles are to be utilized may be functional if it encourages behaviors that are needed for effectiveness, but such selectivity may be dysfunctional if it allows the group to avoid difficult or important issues. It is helpful for the leader to be on the alert for the group's attempts to exert control over member's role behavior, and to stand ready to encourage roles which are useful in the group's work.

SUMMARY

In this chapter we have attempted to provide the reader a short course on group dynamics.[11] Hopefully, by examining the group from several different perspectives you have both gained a feel for group interaction processes and a set of concepts that will be useful in understanding and taking action in operating groups.

We began our cognitive mapping by describing the working group as a *social system* made up of interacting and interrelated parts. A characteristic of such a social system is that its activities encompass the functions of: (a) coping with the environment, (b) performing task activities, (c) expressing and managing feelings, and (d) integrating members into a cohesive system.

In analyzing group behavior it is helpful to separate the *content* or subject matter of the discussion from the *process* or the way in which the group is going about dealing with the content. Common process issues include communication, conflict, and cooperation. The content of a discussion is often related to, and indicative of, underlying process issues. The trained leader will learn to gain insight into the group's process by listening carefully to the content as well as attending to nonverbal cues.

Most groups go through process phases. New groups tend to be concerned about membership and identity while older groups wrestle with problems of decision making and control. Some of the process dynamics are concealed by members because of fears of tarnishing their images. The *Johari window* and the *hidden agenda* are concepts that assist in understanding and coping with incongruities between inner feelings and external behavior.

The *psychological contract* provides a model for looking at the cross-expectations between individual members and the group and for understanding the meaning of membership. The various task, maintenance, and self-oriented behaviors demonstrate some of the characteristic styles with which individuals play out their membership.

LEARNING AIDS

1a. Select a group from the list you developed at the end of Chapter 1. Refer to the 12 C process issues and decide which two or three are most serious and need attention.

1b. Ask other group members to also list their perceptions of the two or three most serious process issues. Run a tally to see which issues are most often mentioned. Discuss these, asking members to give illustrations of how each issue manifests itself.

2. Refer again to the list of groups you developed at the end of Chapter 1. For each group see if you can determine which of the four phases of group development it seems to be working at (membership/acceptance, individual/group goals-needs, communication/decision making, control and organization).

I. _____

II. _____

III. _____

IV. _____

V. _____

VI. _____

VII. _____

VIII. _____

3. A good place to begin working on incongruence in groups is with one's own incongruities. Answer these questions for yourself as honestly as you can.
   A. To what extent am I a person who often says or does things that are quite different from what I feel inside?
   B. In what kinds of settings (groups, etc.) am I most likely to conceal my feelings?
   C. What are the advantages and disadvantages to me of "wearing a mask" and behaving differently than I feel?

4. What, if anything, do you do in groups to cause other people to need to be more incongruent? (i.e., do you ridicule or criticize people for asking questions about things they don't know?) What do you do to help people be more congruent? Discuss your responses with a friend who has seen you operate in groups.

5. Select one of your groups that is important to you. Write out a *psychological contract* that you would like to be able to establish between yourself and the group. Discuss it with the group.

6. In a group meeting have each member keep track of the *task*, *maintenance*, and *individual* roles that he or she plays. At the end of the meeting tally the frequency of the roles for the total group. Are these roles that are overplayed? Underplayed?

NOTES

1. Theodore M. Mills, *The Sociology of Small Groups* (Englewood Cliffs, NJ: Prentice-Hall, 1967).

2. A fuller discussion of this issue is found in L. P. Bradford, D. Stock, and M. Horwitz, "How to Diagnose Group Problems" in *Group Development*, L. P. Bradford, ed. (La Jolla, CA: University Associates, 1978), pp. 62–78.

3. Warren G. Bennis and H. A. Shepard, "A Theory of Group Development," in *Group Development*, L. P. Bradford, ed., pp. 13–35; T. M. Mills, *The Sociology of Small Groups* (Englewood Cliffs, NJ: Prentice Hall, 1967); W. R. Bion, *Experiences in Groups* (New York: Basic Books, 1959).

4. W. C. Schutz, "Interpersonal Underworld," in *The Planning of Change*, W. G. Bennis, K. D. Benne and Robert Chin, eds. (New York: Holt, Rinehart and Winston, 1961).

5. This material is taken from Cyril R. Mill and L. C. Porter, eds., *Reading Book for Laboratories in Human Relations Training* (Washington, D.C.: NTL Institute for Applied Behavioral Science, 1972), pp. 13–14.

6. Joseph Luft, "The JOHARI Window: A Graphic Model of Awareness in Interpersonal Relations," *Human Relations Training News* 5 (1961): 6–7. See also Joseph Luft, *Of Human Interaction* (Palo Alto, CA: National Press Books, 1969).

7. L. P. Bradford, ed., *Group Development* (La Jolla, CA: University Associates, 1978).

8. Edgar H. Schein, *Organizational Psychology* (Englewood Cliffs, NJ: Prentice-Hall, 1965), pp. 10–13, 63–65.

9. Kenneth Benne and P. H. Sheats, "Functional Roles of Group Members," *Journal of Social Issues* 4 (1948): 41–49. Reprinted in L. P. Bradford, ed., *Group Development*.

10. Clovis Shepard, *Small Groups: Some Sociological Perspectives* (San Francisco, CA: Chandler Publishing, 1964), pp. 27–36.

11. For further discussion of applied group dynamics see Joseph Luft, *Group Processes: An Introduction to Group Dynamics*, 3d ed. (Palo Alto, CA: Mayfield Publishing, 1984). Also, A. Paul Hare, *Creativity in Small Groups* (Beverly Hills, CA: Sage Publications, 1982).

5

GROUP LEADERSHIP:
THE PERSON AND THE ROLE

Dean Jones was new to management. He had been promoted from the position of design engineer to chief of the design section. His promotion came about because of his high level of technical performance, his tenure, and his good relationships with his peers. Dean Jones had had little in the way of management training and was worried about how to work effectively with his group. "You have to be tough and decisive—let 'em know who's boss," advised an older supervisor.

"Get to know them as individuals," advised another. "Take them to lunch, find out about their home lives, be their 'father figure.'"

Still another suggested emphasizing teamwork. "Get them working together and maintain the role of coach."

"What's the best approach to group leadership?" Dean wondered. "How do the most effective leaders function? Can I develop an approach that gets the job done and fits my own personality?"

Of all the many topics in the general field of management, more has probably been written about leadership than any other. There are doubtless several reasons for this extensive coverage. In the first place, most of us have an intuitive belief that the leader is the most crucial person in a group or organization. Someone, we presume, must take the leadership position if the system is to control and direct its energy. In addition, many of the consumers of management literature are themselves leaders or would-be leaders. Thus, much is written to appeal to the managerial group. Beyond these obvious factors, there is, I think, a more subtle reason for the emphasis on leadership. Many (probably most) of us are fascinated with leadership and its trappings— power, status, and privilege. For most of us, leadership is not emotionally neutral. We have positive or negative feelings about it. We read novels about great leaders; rarely about great followers. The media call our attention daily to prominent figures in leadership positions. Our own childhood experiences of being controlled and struggling to gain self-control form a foundation for our current preoccupation with leadership.

A common pattern in new or unstructured groups is for several individuals to make strong moves for leadership. If the bids are rejected by other members there often follows a period when leadership in the group is suspect and no one will risk exerting any direction. On the other hand, if the leadership bid is done smoothly and succeeds, the new leader(s) are greeted with mixed feelings by the other members. While it is a relief to have someone in a position to assume responsibility, there are also fears that the leader(s) will move the group in undesirable directions. Often these fears build into countermoves to control the leader.

The point of this discussion is to remind the reader that leadership is not a benign and totally rational topic. It is not like studying the steps in a logical problem-solving model. Experiencing and discussing leadership arouses in both leaders and followers such significant human concerns as manipulation, potency, democracy, distribution of power, punishment, and personal integrity. The study of leadership makes evident to the leader the need to take a look at herself and to make choices about the fit between personal strengths, values, leadership strategies, and situations. There are no certain strategies for success as a leader, the popular management literature not withstanding. There are, however, some fairly reliable formulas for failure.

In this chapter we will review a few of the more widely accepted and useful ideas about leadership and attempt to provide some guidelines for group leadership strategies and personal leadership styles.

WHAT IS LEADERSHIP?

One of the things that makes leadership difficult to study in a coherent fashion is the large number of ways in which the term is used.

In order to talk about approaches to leadership effectiveness in groups there are some basic distinctions that first must be clarified.

One of the confusions has to do with *formal* versus *informal* (or emergent) leadership. The boss who sits at the head of the table or the appointed chairperson of a meeting is the formal leader. His leadership (or at least authority) is based on a formal role as designated by higher powers. Such leaders do not have to *do* anything to gain the role. The informal leader, on the other hand, emerges from the group and gains influence because of her behavior and the perceptions of the others. Informal leaders usually are accepted by the group because it is perceived that they can help members meet their needs. For example, in a group in which the formally designated leader is weak, members may become frustrated with the lack of progress. At that stage a member who is vocal, who has ideas about what needs to be done, and who is reasonably well liked and trusted may become a major guiding force—the real, though "informal" leader. Such leadership may continue to exert a significant force unless it is challenged by the formal leaders or by other informal leaders with their own "program" for meeting group members' needs.

The focus of this book is primarily on the formal leader and what he can do to be effective. It should be clear, however, that informal leadership processes are also of major significance in a work group setting. Even in situations in which there is a designated leader, acts of leadership, both positive and negative, may be carried out by other members. That is, members may behave in ways that will influence others to follow their suggestions, adopt their points of view, and move in a particular direction. Such behavior may be in support of or in opposition to the formal leader. It is this reality of shared leadership that has led group theorists to point out that group leadership can most accurately be thought of as a process rather than as a specific person in a role. This perspective allows the formal leader to ask, "Within this framework of shared leadership and influence, what part can I play that will help move the group in effective directions?"

THE POWER OF THE LEADER

It needs to be clearly understood at the outset that group leadership, both formal and informal, operates on the basis of *power*. Power in social systems relates to human need satisfaction. It may consist of raw power, the ability to fire someone or take away their privileges. Or it may take a more subtle form and be termed influence or leverage. In any case, however, it deals with one individual's ability to affect another by influencing the degree to which the other's needs are satisfied or frustrated.

Power shows up in several different forms and may be applied in different ways. French and Raven, in their studies of power, have identified five categories that apply to the exertion of power in groups.[1]

- *Reward power.* The capacity to offer rewards (money, recognition, position, etc.) to persons in order to influence them to behave in a certain way.

- *Punishment power or coercion.* Capacity to influence others' behavior by threatening unpleasant outcomes unless they obey.

- *Legitimate power or position power.* Capacity to influence the behavior of others because of the prerogative of the office or role one holds within the organization structure.

- *Expert power.* Capacity to influence others because of knowledge about the situation that the others do not have, or have in lesser degrees.

- *Referent power.* Capacity to influence others by generating in them a liking for or respect of the leader as a person (charisma).

Most leaders have more than one of these kinds of power, and of course the amount available varies from time to time and situation to situation. It is important to determine carefully what kinds and how much power one has before attempting to lead. It is also important to distinguish the requirements of the situation from one's own internal needs for power and control.

THE SHARING OF POWER

The basic dilemma in modern leadership is how much power should be held by the leader and how much should be shared with members. The range of choices is illustrated in Figure 5.1.

FIGURE 5.1

Leader Domination	Shared Power	Member Domination
(Total Autocracy)		(Pure Democracy)

As indicated, the choices run (in theory at least) from total leader domination to member domination. Such extremes, however, are unlikely because, on the one hand (as Machiavelli pointed out in *The Prince*), few leaders can maintain their power for long without the "consent of the governed," and on the other hand, if any group were totally devoid of formal leadership, informal leadership would emerge or the group would dissolve. Nonetheless, within the range of possibilities there is room for the leader to choose an approach.

The prototype for the group with complete leader domination is provided by Freud's "primal horde." He hypothesized that at early stages of civilization human organization was characterized by chieftains who had virtually complete domination over their members. In return for his strength and protection, individuals gave the leader control not only of their behavior, but also of their feelings and even their individuality. The leader's needs took precedence over all others. Through the influence of the leader, the thoughts and feelings of members were molded into a single "group psychology." The leader had, or was reputed to have, all of the five modes of power described by French and Raven. The extreme control over need-satisfying behavior, including sexual expression, forced members into a strong emotional dependency on the leader, often at the unconscious level. This ambivalence (coexisting positive and negative feelings) about leadership continues to exist in many contemporary groups. Perhaps the best example of the primal horde in present society is the cult that grows up around a charismatic religious leader who encourages members to rid themselves of present and future bad feelings by submerging their personalities and needs in the movement.

Examples of the opposite of the primal horde are almost completely democratic egalitarian groups in which most of the control is vested in the members and the leader serves "at the pleasure" of the others. Thus a group of people with a common interest (photography, a political cause, a community issue) might come together as equals and elect officers in order to coordinate activities. Another example is the T-Group or sensitivity-training group in which, under specified conditions of time and procedure, leaderless and unstructured training groups are formed for purposes of exploring individual and group development. It should be noted that even in groups in which the psychological contract regarding democratic leadership is clearly drawn, there is still likely to be mistrust and jealousy regarding leadership because of our deeply buried feelings about control.

Between the two extremes of leader versus member power lie most of the alternatives one encounters in real-life managerial situations. A good deal of current management theory aims at helping the leader choose the most effective mix of leader and member power.

Traditional management theory held that "ownership" of the group or organization and its attendant reward, punishment, and positional power called for highly authoritarian leadership. The leader presided over a command system in which orders were issued from the top of the hierarchy, and people at the bottom were expected to comply unquestionly. The assumption was that expert power was automatically correlated with the other forms of power, (i.e., that those in charge knew best because they were in charge).

Douglas McGregor suggested that the rationale for the authoritarian approach lay in the implicit assumptions that traditional managers made about their subordinates' motivation. These Theory X assumptions were that workers were inherently lazy and wanted to avoid work, that they cared nothing about the organization's needs, that they wished to avoid responsibility, and that they needed to be strongly controlled in order to produce.[2] This set of assumptions probably meshed fairly well with the societal values and realities of the nineteenth and early twentieth centuries, when strong emphasis on legitimate authority was widely accepted. The masses were not well educated and many were fresh from rural backgrounds. There were few welfare programs to augment the job in meeting human needs. Industrialism and capitalism were heralded as the keys to improved quality of life. The industrial manager—the "captain of industry"—was a folk hero saluted by Horatio Alger and others. The leader stereotype was that of the traditionally masculine figure—strong, completely under control, cool and calculating, aggressive, and a cut above the followers.

By the 1930s doubts began to grow about the overall effectiveness of the authoritarian style of management. The Hawthorne Studies, mentioned earlier, were the first wave of a spate of research projects that demonstrated the impact on employee performance of attitudes, social processes, and work group norms. Industrialists such as Chester Barnard documented the approaches of effective managers whose techniques went far beyond just issuing commands.[3] At the same time societal values began to shift away from unquestioned acceptance of authority toward asking why? and demanding that leaders demonstrate expert power to go along with their position power. Workers became better educated and more independent as employment alternatives and welfare programs developed. McGregor's Theory Y, the assumption that under some circumstances workers might desire to work, seek responsibility, care about the organization, and operate under self-control, gained credibility as an option for managers. After World War II the pendulum of U.S. management thinking swung for many away from the authoritarian model to the democratic model. Managers took courses in human relations, learned to ask rather than demand, covered the iron fist with a velvet glove, and hired consultants to help install participative management programs.

At the present writing the pendulum of the authoritarianism–democracy arc appears to have swung back to a middle position. Highly democratic management is not possible in all situations, nor is it always effective. Some employees do not respond well to democratic management, probably because of their personality structures and/or past lessons as subordinates. Some leaders who have tried to initiate democratic methods in the midst of a highly authoritarian organization have been badly disappointed. Contemporary researchers have devised "contingency theories" to help leaders identify circumstances under which various degrees of sharing of power would be most effective. We will discuss these contingency theories later in this chapter, after having first discussed leadership styles.

The manager who, as a part of her role, is leader of one or more face-to-face groups, is confronted with some considerations about the use of power that are somewhat different from those of the upper-level executive who controls large numbers of staff members through procedures, memoranda, or delegation. For the group leader the smaller, more initimate grouping and more intensive ongoing interaction raise additional problems. For one thing, the leader is highly visible. His competence, dependability, congruence, honesty, and emotional responses are almost impossible to keep hidden. Some group leaders attempt to use high levels of authoritarianism to cover up their lack of personal competence, commitment, or integrity.

Such tactics are, in my experience, virtually always painfully apparent to group members. The leader may be obeyed (usually in the letter but not in the spirit of the law) but is not respected. Other leaders attempt to cover up the same set of inadequacies by the appearance of a highly democratic and participative system that they control by making all significant decisions ahead of time and subtly selling them to group members. Such a ruse is seen through more quickly than most manipulative leaders suspect, and causes loss of respect. At a later point, we will discuss some strategies for choosing the most effective distributions of power under varying circumstances. At this stage we suggest a point of view regarding *how* one exercises whatever power distribution is chosen. It is usually best to be straightforward and clear about how much power you intend to share or not share; if possible, say why. Keep your approach authentic, consistent, and goal oriented. Don't falsely raise employee expectations or change signals on them. Such behavior demoralizes and immobilizes people. They don't know what is expected of them and may become frustrated and willing to follow the leader's wishes only through threat of punishment.

LEADERSHIP STYLES

The term leadership style has taken on a particular meaning within the framework of current applied research. In the pioneering studies conducted at Ohio State University Bureau of Business Research in the 1950s, analyses of the behavior of hundreds of leaders were conducted in order to isolate the major dimensions of leadership.[4] Two factors were identified that subsumed most of the leader behaviors. One factor contained *task-oriented* behaviors (originally called "initiating structure") aimed exclusively at getting the job done. The second factor contained *people-oriented* behaviors (originally called "consideration") and referred to acts designed to help people meet their needs.

Task-oriented behaviors characterize leadership activity that relates directly to work procedures, organization of duties, and goal attainment, and usually operate at the content level. The task-oriented leader would tend to devote energy to getting work done by the following style:

● Establishing rules, procedures, and by-laws;

● Clearly specifying roles and tasks for members and evaluating performance;

● Spelling out the relationships between leader and members on the basis of prerogatives and responsibilities;

● Delimiting channels of communication and decision-making procedures.

People-oriented behaviors are aimed at getting work done by creating positive feelings and commitment among members. The following activities characterize such a style:

● Behaving in a friendly manner toward members and encouraging them to behave the same way;

● Striving to create an atmosphere of mutual support and trust;

● Being available for counsel and lending a sympathetic ear to members;

● Encouraging members to contribute suggestions and demonstrating willingness to make changes.

For a while there were debates about which style of leadership was most effective ("Should you be people-oriented or task-oriented?"). Further investigation demonstrated that the two dimensions are not mutually exclusive (see Figure 5.2). It is possible to be high on both (cell a), low on both (cell c), or high on one and low on the other (cells b and d).

Robert Blake and Jane Mouton have adapted the material into a training framework called the Managerial Grid.[5] Managers fill out a questionnaire and/or are rated by colleagues to find out where they score on the task- and people-orientation dimensions. It is the belief of Blake and Mouton, based on experience with large numbers of managers, that the high-task, high-people position is usually most effective (referred to as 9/9 or Team Management). The assumption is that good managers can operate so as to maximize both aspects;

FIGURE 5.2 LEADERSHIP STYLES

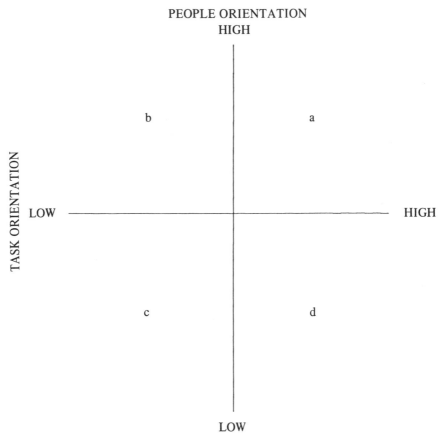

they do not have to choose between one or the other. This point of view has been appealing and useful to managers who have wondered whether it is better to be tough-minded (task-oriented, demanding, evaluative) or tender-minded (people-oriented, supportive, delegating). The answer from the leadership style researchers is that you do not have to choose between the two; you can do both. Further, you do not have to compromise by settling for modest amounts of each if you are skillful enough with the maintenance of the social system while at the same time stressing efficiency and goal attainment. We will discuss this balancing act again in a later section on the contingency approach.

GROUP CLIMATE AS A CONTEXT FOR LEADERSHIP

Another perspective on leadership impact has been provided by those who have studied the climate or emotional atmosphere of groups. A leader may, by his behavior, help set a tone for the group that significantly affects interaction and work. (Of course other members, in addition to the formal leader, also contribute to the climate.) An interesting series of studies on climate and leadership was reported by Gibb.[6] By recording the discussions of a variety of groups over several years he was able to sort group behavioral characteristics into the two categories of *defensive* and *supportive* climates, as shown below (see Table 5.1).

TABLE 5.1. Categories of behavioral characteristic of supportive and defensive climates in small groups

Defensive climates	Supportive climates
Evaluation	Description
Control	Problem orientation
Strategy	Spontaneity
Neutrality	Empathy
Superiority	Equality
Certainty	Provisionalism

The dynamics of the defensive climate have to do with the perceived threat in the group and members' actions to protect themselves. When the behavior of the leader is such that people feel they are being continually evaluated, controlled, and strategized against, and when the leader seems unconcerned about members' welfare, connotes feelings of superiority, and appears dogmatic and unwilling to bend, a significant amount of members' energy is expended in working on defenses rather than on the task. (In Chapter 2 we discussed group members' needs to protect themselves against disconfirmation and loss of self-esteem.)

Gibb's findings are that a supportive climate is characterized by leader and member behavior that seeks to gather information to describe what happened rather than evaluate it, to engage in mutual problem solving rather than control and manipulation, and to behave straightforwardly and spontaneously rather than strategically. The supportive climate also involves empathy and appreciation among leader and members, feelings of mutual respect, equality as human beings regardless of differences in skill or status, and provisionalism in the sense of openness to other points of view and flexibility if the data indicate a need to change.

The term climate seems an appropriate description of the phenomena Gibb describes, because the behavioral characteristics within each list become self-perpetuating. That is, controlling, evaluative behavioral styles increase defensiveness, which in turn encourages more strategizing, and so on. On the other hand, nonthreatening, open, and supportive behaviors lower the need for defenses and encourage more spontaneity and flexibility. Once a climate is established, especially a defensive one, it is difficult to change. Even if they want to behave differently, members understand that they undertake significant risks when they give up strategizing and neutrality in favor of more spontaneity and openness. Unless all members and the leader are *really* going to behave according to new ground rules, a single member who tries to change (drop her defenses) is vulnerable to embarrassment and loss of self-esteem.

Argyris developed a procedure for observing and recording managerial meetings in organizations and analyzing the proceedings according to a set of categories that relate also to the concept of climate.[7] In Argyris's framework the following categories of behavior are important in maintaining an effective social system:

1. Receiving and giving nonevaluative descriptive feedback about the performance and mutual impact of oneself and others;

2. "Owning" (owning up to or admitting to the existence of) and permitting others to openly admit their ideas, feelings, and values;

3. Openness to new ideas, feelings, and values and permitting others to experience the same;

4. Willingness to experiment and take risks with new ideas, feelings, and values.

In organizations that are characterized by (a) task orientation to the point of devaluing human relationships, (b) a highly rational–

logical style with little room for emotionality, and (c) high degrees of coercion and control, the effectiveness begins to decrease, and the opposite state of affairs occurs. When feedback becomes evaluative, there is disowning and closed communication; and when experimentation and risk taking fall off, there develops a low level of *interpersonal competence* in the organization. Its consequences include mistrust, conformity, defensiveness, and low commitment.

The findings of Gibb and Argyris are complementary and direct the leader to another aspect of group life on which leadership behavior impacts. The social-emotional climate of the group may act to block expression and creativity or it may support and encourage them. Available energy can be used toward playing task and maintenance roles or toward building defenses and playing protective games.

CONTINGENCIES IN CHOOSING
A LEADERSHIP STRATEGY

So far, we have discussed a variety of alternative strategies for exerting leadership, including the forms of power one uses and how much is shared with members, leadership style (task versus people orientation), and climate. It would be convenient to be able to specify a set of behaviors from those we have discussed that are guaranteed to work under all circumstances. Unfortunately, as we have learned before, dealing with human behavior is not that simple. Some of the popular writers to the contrary, current evidence is that no single approach works in all situations. Leadership researchers have recently busied themselves with studying the *situational* influences on leadership performance and attempting to specify the *contingencies* under which a given approach functions best.

Fielder has identified three major situational variables that affect the effectiveness of a given approach to leadership.[8] These are:

• The *position power* of the leader. The power available to the leader because of what the organization vests in the position. Generally, these would be the French and Raven power sources of reward, punishment, and position power. (Expert and referent power are largely personal rather than situational.)

• The degree of *structuredness of the task.* Whether the work to be done by the group is highly controlled and specified (assembling products from components) or general and open-ended (handling citizen complaints).

• *Quality of relationship* with members. Is there appreciation and rapport between leader and members?

These three variables may occur in any combination in a given situation. For example, a given leader may have good relations with members, be operating in an unstructured situation, and have very little power, perhaps as a popular chairperson of a citizens' committee on programs for the elderly. Or the leader may have good relations with members in a highly structured work setting with high position power, possibly in a relationship-oriented supervisor in a bookkeeping section. The most favorable group situation with regard to the amount of influence the leader can exert is one in which he has high position power, a clear-cut task to perform, and is well liked by the members. The most unfavorable situation, then, involves an unpopular leader with low position power and an ill-defined task.

Fiedler investigated the relative effectiveness of the two major leadership styles we have discussed (task-oriented and people-oriented). His findings indicate that task-oriented leaders usually function most effectively in either very favorable or very unfavorable situations, as described in the paragraph above. People-oriented leaders, on the other hand, tend to perform best in mixed situations intermediate between the most and least favorable, where they have moderate power and a somewhat structured task. The findings clearly demonstrate that situational aspects of the leader's role are important in determining which leadership style will be most effective.

Other leadership researchers have brought additional situational variables into the picture. Vroom has contributed substantially to an approach to managerial decision making referred to as *contingency theory*.[9] Contingency theory is an outcome of the evidence, such as that from Fiedler, that no one leadership style works best in all situations.[10] The situational variables identified by Vroom and Yetton are as follows:

1. The *quality* of the decision. Is the situation such that the correct solution is likely to be of significantly greater effectiveness than the other alternatives (for example, selecting a plan for reducing cost

over-runs). Or will any of the feasible solutions work about equally well, except for possible variations in member acceptance or time involved (establishing a format for a written report, choosing sub-committees, etc.).

2. Does the leader possess enough information to make a good decision, or do data and expertise need to be acquired from others?

3. Is the problem structured or unstructured?

4. Is acceptance of the decision by members necessary in order to obtain effective implementation?

5. Are members likely to accept a decision that the leader makes by herself?

6. Do members share the organization's goals in this problem-solving situation?

7. Are members likely to be in conflict over preferred solutions?

Vroom and Yetton provide a schematic "decision tree" whereby a leader may analyze any situation and select an appropriate style, ranging from a completely unilateral and authoritarian approach to a participative group decision. The complete model has been used extensively to train managers in contingency approaches to leadership (a worthwhile learning experience for any manager). It is difficult to boil down all the options in the decision tree into a simple statement. For our purposes Vroom and Yetton's findings demonstrate that in situations in which (a) member acceptance of actions or decisions is important, (b) the leader has incomplete information or expertise, (c) conflict is a likelihood, and (d) members share the goals, the participative approaches are most effective. More unilateral styles work well in (a) structured situations where the leader has the information, (b) where member acceptance or agreement is not necessary or likely, and (c) when time is short. Thus, the leader who is searching for an effective style may change strategies, depending on the characteristics of the situation and the members.

There are several risks in attempting to summarize and integrate the finding about the impact of the climate and situations on choices of leadership style and power sharing. For one thing, the findings of the research to which we have referred are couched in terms of probabilities and trends; they hold true much of the time but are not infallible. Second, the various studies were conducted in different groups under different circumstances. Their findings, therefore, may may not fit together perfectly. And finally, an additional source of error creeps in when the leader seeks to apply the ideas gleaned from research. There are both skill and value considerations involved; you and I might behave quite differently from each other in our attempts to be task-oriented, benevolent autocrats. After establishing these several caveats we will proceed to propose some guidelines for choosing an approach to group leadership.

Most groups, in operating organizations that the readers of this book encounter, have not attained the ideal supportive and interpersonally effective climates described by Gibb and Argyris. These are goals, not realities. There is usually a certain degree of distrust, closed communication, game playing, and manipulation. Process issues stemming from relationship problems are likely to go unrecognized and not be dealt with. Thus, it is probably best to work up gradually to highly democratic/participative approaches. Members are likely to want some initial structure and control.

In situations in which the leader is powerful and knowledgeable about the problem and the task is structured, but where the members are not committed and their acceptance is not crucial, an authoritarian and task-centered approach appears to work quite well, at least in the short run.

On the other hand, when the leader's power to command compliance is limited; member contributions, acceptance, and implementation are important; and the task somewhat unstructured, a leadership approach that builds the relationship as well as the task aspects of the group and moves toward greater participation is probably advisable.

The preponderance of evidence seems to be that, in the long run, it is desirable to work in the direction of developing a more supportive, participative group with people and task orientations integrated, especially if member contributions and creativity are important aspects of effectiveness. Such an effort takes time and considerable commitment from the leadership and membership. It should be evident by now that the internal workings of a group are the result of a myriad of factors that cannot be changed quickly and easily, and that an important aspect of the leader's role is "climate building."

LEADERSHIP SKILLS

In addition to the considerations of style and climate, it is possible to consider the *skills* necessary to effective group leadership. That is, we may ask, "What skills in dealing with people in groups do effective leaders seem to have?" Although situations vary considerably, some fairly strong indicators emerge from the literature.

The Leader As Diagnostician

Schein in his writings on management makes a case for the importance of diagnostic skills. Other views of management agree. One cannot select a strategy and chart a course of action without a clear understanding of the significant aspects of the situation. It is my view that the manager who operates as a group leader can most usefully adopt a practical version of the scientific method called "action research." The action research model requires that the leader be both an active participant and a detached analyst.[11] As action researcher, the leader continually cycles through the following steps:

• Gathers information about the ongoing interaction process through careful observation or other data-gathering techniques such as questionnaires.

• Fits the data into a framework or theory designed to help make sense out of it (such as the models described in this book)

• Arrives at a tentative diagnosis of what is happening (a hypothesis).

• Tests that diagnosis by using himself as an instrument of intervention to affect the situation.

• Evaluates the impact of the intervention to either confirm or refute the diagnosis.

• Begins the process over again.

Functioning as an effective diagnostician is a skill, or rather a set of skills. It involves understanding of process issues (which we will discuss further in the next chapter) and the ability to bring such issues to the attention of the group in a minimally threatening way so that they can be productively worked on.

Likert's "New Patterns"

In the ongoing research at the University of Michigan's Institute for Social Research, Rensis Likert and his colleagues compared the behavior of successful and unsuccessful managers.[12] Some of the factors that described successful managers had to do with group leadership behavior. According to Likert;

The superiors who have the most favorable and cooperative attitudes in their work groups display the following characteristics:

> The attitude and behavior of the superior toward the subordinate as a person, *as perceived by the subordinate* is as follows:
>
> He is supportive, friendly, and helpful rather than hostile. He is kind but firm, never threatening, genuinely interested in the well-being of subordinates and endeavors to treat people in a sensitive, considerate way. He is just, if not generous. He endeavors to serve the best interests of his employees as well as of the company.
>
> He shows confidence in the integrity, ability, and motivations of subordinates rather than suspicion and distrust.
>
> His confidence in subordinates leads him to have high expectations as to their level of performance. With confidence that he will not be disappointed, he expects much, not little. (This, again, is fundamentally a supportive rather than a critical or hostile relationship.)
>
> He sees that each subordinate is well trained for his particular job. He endeavors also to help subordinates be promoted by training them for jobs at the next level. This involves giving them relevant experience and coaching whenever the opportunity offers.
>
> He coaches and assists employees whose performance is below standard. In the case of a subordinate who is clearly misplaced and unable to do his job satisfactorily, he endeavors to find a position well suited to that employee's abilities and arranges to have employee transferred to it.

The behavior of the superior in directing work is characterized by such activity as:

Planning and scheduling the work to be done, training subordinates, supplying them with material and tools, initiating work activity, etc.

Providing adequate technical competence, particularly in those situations where the work has not been highly standardized.

The leader develops his subordinates into a working team with high group loyalty by using participation and the other kinds of group leadership practices. . . .

Interpersonal Competence

In most leadership roles, skill in human interaction is important. This skill is labeled by some as interpersonal competence. It involves sensitivity to others' ideas and feelings and to oneself. One group of authors defines interpersonal competence as the capacity to function in five areas:

1. Capacity to receive and send information and feelings reliably. This includes the usual two-way communication (sending/listening) skills, but also awareness of and sensitivity to others.

2. Capacity to evoke expressions of feeling. Ability to help other people feel free to express thoughts, beliefs, and feelings openly.

3. Capacity to process information and feelings reliably and creatively. The ability to understand and make sense out of (diagnose) interactions with and among others.

4. Capacity to implement a course of action. Skills to take operational steps to improve interactions, solve problems, and create new structures.

5. Capacity to learn in each of the above areas. A combination of skills, including staying flexible and open to new learning, continually analyzing one's experience, and modifying, when appropriate, one's views, techniques, and styles.[13]

Other Group Leadership Skills

Probably every group leader and every student of groups has her own list of essential skills. The following is my list. It is not meant to be exhaustive (though perhaps exhausting) and, again, the importance of each skill varies, depending on group situations.

• *Interpersonal competence.* We have already discussed this skill. Generally, it involves sensitivity to others' ideas and feelings and the ability to interact so that all members of the group (including the leader) feel encouraged and supported in their participation.

• *Communication skills.* Effective communication is, of course, closely allied with interpersonal competence. We set it apart here for emphasis. Good communication includes the willingness and ability to listen to what others say as well as getting one's own message across.

• *Problem-solving skills.* The ability to help a group define, analyze, and solve problems. We will discuss this topic in detail in Chapter 7.

• *Ability to cope with conflict.* Conflict is an inherent part of human existence because we have different needs, goals, perceptions, and affiliations. The effective leader needs to learn not to freeze up, run away psychologically, or sweep conflicts under the rug when they arise. Neither is it usually helpful to stamp out arguments.

• *Timing.* Good timing is important in group leadership, as it is in many other endeavors. It is easy to spot bad timing, as in the case of the leader who cuts people off too soon or waits too long to silence the bore, or pushes for a decision before the group is ready. The problem is that it is very difficult to tell someone how to have good timing. Probably the crucial issue in timing is readiness. Is the group ready to move to another topic? Are the members ready to listen to feedback about their performance? Good timing involves an intuitive sense of the psychological state of group members. It can best be learned by careful observation of whether one's inputs fall on fertile ground and help the group along or whether they have a negative effect or no effect at all.

CAN LEADERS CHANGE THEIR STYLES?

It is one thing to cite studies that describe the skills and styles of effective leaders and quite another to expect a specific leader to drop her old behaviors and adopt a new repertoire. Research on management development and transfer of learning clearly demonstrates that learning new concepts and practices does not necessarily mean that those concepts and practices will be successfully applied.

One reason that what is learned is not necessarily implemented has to do with resistances in the situation. In a classic study by Fleishman, managers were taken out of their corporate setting and provided intensive training in human relations skills.[14] Evaluations at the end of the program demonstrated that the trainees had gained new perspectives and attitudes. However, follow-up research indicated that once back in the work setting, supervisors' attitudes reverted to pretraining levels or worse. The many factors that had not changed—their superiors' attitudes, workers' expectations, established practices, rules and regulations—had counteracted the effects of the training. This phenomenon has been noted many times since. Likewise, the group leader who gains new skills can meet significant resistances when he first attempts to apply them in an ongoing group in an organization. Members are likely to exert subtle pressures to bring things back to "normal."

I once had a student who was supervisor of a work group in a large corporation. During a course on group behavior he decided to try out some of the ideas in his unit. He later reported to me that, "These group dynamics ideas don't work in the real world." He explained to his group (apparently in very few words) that he wanted some changes—more discussion, more participation in the decision making, and more self-direction by the group. Then, "The group just sat there and didn't say anything for five minutes and I had to move in and take over."

Another source of difficulty in applying new learning resides within the leader. Argyris has found that for many people there is a discrepancy between our "espoused theories" (the behavioral strategies we *say* we pursue) and our "theory-in-use" (the approach we actually use).[15] The reasons for this discrepancy are lack of clear feedback in most situations about the impact of our behavior on others and a fairly common set of implicit beliefs about the necessity of an individualistic, win/lose, rational, nonemotional stance in interpersonal situations. Argyris's work leads us to predict that the readers of this book, like other leaders, see themselves as more egalitarian and people oriented than they are and more than their subordinates think they are. This is partly because you frequently get very little feedback about your behavior (others fear angering you and having to suffer consequences) and also because you are likely to have a set of beliefs (often unarticulated) about the need for a control-oriented, win/lose approach.

The purpose of this section is to remind the reader of the difficulties of applying learning about groups to real situations. There are remedies for dealing with the situational resistances to training. These include involving managers at all levels in the organization in the training process, moving the training out of the classroom and into the workplace (organization development and related practices), and follow-up coaching and support for trainees as they attempt to apply their lessons. A variety of training programs are available to assist in overcoming the gap between what we do and what we think we do. Such programs may utilize questionnaires to diagnose leadership styles and various simulated group tasks and feedback techniques to assist in self-understanding.[16]

VALUE CHOICES IN THE LEADERSHIP

An issue in the application of leadership styles and practices that is not given enough attention is that of values. Whatever set of choices one makes in regard to a personal leadership approach had better square with his value system. Otherwise, one is likely to find himself under constant tension. If you have a deep-seated belief in democratic principles and a sympathetic, people-oriented approach to groups you will probably find it stressful to try to become more aggressive and controlling. If you have behind you a work history of experiences as a power-oriented, unilateral manager, do not expect yourself to move comfortably to become more participative and people oriented until you have examined your own values and found yourself to be ready to change them. And if you don't like to work closely with people, but believe in the integrity of the skilled craftsman or bench scientist, think twice before you accept a job as group leader. Trying to be something that you are not is not only stressful but often is seen through by members.

One of the most potent value issues in groups has to do with manipulation. This threatening word means to most people a process whereby we are influenced in such a way that (a) we have no control over what is happening and (b) we don't know it is happening. Every once in a while I have a student in a course who says that her goal is to "learn to manipulate others." Such an assertion is met with icy gazes and fidgets by other class members. No one wants to be manipulated in the sense that we have used the term. Those whose value systems accept manipulation as a viable leadership tool are well advised to either revise their values or figure out how to gain considerable power. Manipulation is nearly always seen through sooner or later and stands as an open invitation for retaliation.

There are other value issues in the group leader's role. Many of these were raised in Chapter 3. They have to do with such factors as expression of feelings, competition, male and female roles, and structure. Again, where one stands on these various value dimensions has a strong influence on how well a given style or leadership skill fits. It also, of course, has a strong influence on one's tendency to judge a given approach as "bad" or "wrong" or "ineffective" when it does not agree with one's values. Thus, an understanding of one's own values and their impact on one's behavior in groups is an important element of successful leadership.

SUMMARY

In this chapter, we have covered a great deal of ground in relation to the question, "What makes an effective group leader?" We have seen that a variety of styles, power orientations, skills and values go into the leadership mix, and that the formula for leadership effectiveness varies from one kind of situation to another. We have stressed a diagnostic approach in which the leader gathers all the information available to arrive at a strategy which best fits both his own skills and values and the characteristics of the situation.

It is well to remember a point made early in the chapter, that leadership in groups is a *process* and does not rest with a single individual. Unless a leader is in the unlikely situation of being able to exert complete control over the group, there is a sharing of leadership, information, and responsibilities. The formal leader's challenge is the five-fold task of (a) keeping the group moving in the direction of the task or decision; (b) maintaining member morale and commitment; (c) drawing on the energy and resources of the members; (d) developing the group as an operating system that can continue to function effectively; and (e) maintaining her own satisfaction and equanimity in the situation.

LEARNING AIDS

1. For those groups you selected at the end of Chapter 1 decide:
   A. In which do you have a *formal* leadership role, and in which is your leadership *informal*?
   B. For each group in both categories determine which of the French and Raven types of power goes along with your role.
      Reward power
      Punishment power
      Legitimate or position power
      Expert power
      Referent power/personal charisma

2. A. For the groups above in which you have a *formal* leadership role, which of the following power distributions best fits you in your own perception. Select a number from 1 to 4 or any fraction between.
      1. Exploitative/authoritative
      2. Benevolent/authoritative
      3. Consultative
      4. Participative/group decision
   B. What number would your *group members* assign you on the 1 to 4 scale in each of these groups (You may wish to ask them.)

3. A. As a general pattern do you see yourself as:

   _____ High on people orientation, low on task orientation.

   _____ Low on people orientation, high on task orientation.

   _____ High on both people and task orientation.

   _____ Moderate on both people and task orientation.

   _____ Low on both people and task orientation.

    B. Think of an example of a recent leadership situation that illustrates your rating of yourself in 3A.

4. Select the group from your list that has the *most defensive climate.*
    A. Describe the behaviors that occur in this group that are indicative of a defensive climate.
    B. What factors can you identify that contribute to the defensiveness of the group climate? (If you do not belong to a group with a defensive climate, select one with a supportive climate.)

5. Based on the discussion of the *skills* of effective leaders, make a list of the skills you believe you need to acquire to become more effective as a group leader.

6. Do you have any strong values about issues related to group leadership that would affect your ability to adopt a particular style or power orientation? (It might be helpful to think about whether you tend to get into conflict with others over the conduct of meetings, the leader's role, etc.)

7. In your current group leadership situations are there any that you find particularly frustrating or dissatisfying? If so, can you identify some of the causes? (For example, are your needs being thwarted?)

NOTES

1. J. R. P. French, Jr. and B. Raven, "The Bases of Social Power," in *Studies in Social Power*, D. Cartwright, ed. (Ann Arbor, MI: Institute for Social Research, 1959). Reprinted in *Group Dynamics: Research and Theory*, 3d ed., D. Cartwright and A. Zander, eds., (New York: Harper and Row, 1968).

2. Douglas McGregor, *The Human Side of Enterprise* (New York: McGraw-Hill, 1960).

3. Chester Barnard, *Functions of the Executive* (Cambridge, MA: Harvard University Press, 1948).

4. R. M. Stogdill and C. L. Shartle, *Methods in the Study of Administrative Leadership* (Columbus, OH: Ohio State University Bureau of Business Research, 1956).

5. Robert R. Blake and Jane S. Mouton, *The Managerial Grid* (Houston, TX: Gulf Publishing, 1964).

6. Jack R. Gibb, "Defensive Communication," *Journal of Communication* 11 (1961): 141–48.

7. Chris Argyris, *Interpersonal Competence and Organizational Effectiveness* (Homewood, IL: Richard D. Irvin, 1962).

8. Fred E. Fiedler, *A Theory of Leadership Effectiveness* (New York: McGraw-Hill, 1967).

9. Victor H. Vroom and P. Yetton, *Leadership and Decision-Making* (Pittsburgh, PA: University of Pittsburgh Press, 1973).

10. Edgar Schein, *Organizational Psychology* (Englewood Cliffs, NJ: Prentice-Hall, 1965).

11. Neely Gardner, "Action-Training and Research: Something Old and Something New," *Public Administration Review* 34 (1974): 106–15.

12. Likert, *New Patterns of Management*, p. 101.

13. W. G. Bennis, E. H. Schein, F. I. Steele, and D. E. Berlow, *Interpersonal Dynamics: Essays and Readings in Human Interaction* (Homewood, IL: Dorsey Press, 1968), pp. 670–72.

14. Edwin A. Fleishman, "Leadership Climate, Human Relations Training and Supervisory Behavior," *Personnel Psychology* 6 (1953): 205–22.

15. Chris Argyris, "Leadership, Learning and Changing the Status Quo," *Organizational Dynamics* (Winter 1976): 29–43.

16. For a thorough discussion of group leadership for managers by one field's senior authorities, see Alvin Zander, *Making Groups Effective* (San Francisco, CA: Jossey-Bass, 1982).

6

COPING WITH GROUP
PROCESS ISSUES

The president's "cabinet" (the vice-presidents and other top-echelon officers) met weekly to monitor the firm's progress. The meetings were devoted to reviewing programs, analyzing reports, and solving problems that cut across the divisions. The sessions were a crucial aspect of the president's managerial strategy. No single individual had the experience and expertise to deal with the issues that arose. It was essential that the group function effectively as a team.

In order to help assure that the maximum level of teamwork was achieved, the president asked Sally Scott, director of personnel, to sit in the meetings as "process observer." Sally's job was to observe the group and point out problems in their functioning that they might improve. Although Sally had a background in personnel, she had never consulted with a team. "What factors shall I look for," she wondered. "And how can I help the group deal with them?"

In Chapter 4 we described the fundamental distinction between the *content* and *process* aspects of group activity. Content, you will remember, refers to the substance, or the *what*, of the task discussion—the problem on the loading dock, the sales goal for next quarter, a new technique for building a widget. Process refers to *how* the group members are working together in dealing with the content (disagreements, confusion, competitiveness, etc.). Process involves patterns of interaction as members deal overtly or covertly with social-emotional issues that affect work on the task. Understanding and coping with group process issues is one of the major ways in which a leader can help the group improve both its performance and its satisfaction.

In this chapter we will discuss in more detail the 12 process issues that were introduced in Chapter 4 and provide some suggestions for dealing with them. Such an aspiration is a little risky for several reasons. First, all the answers about how to resolve process problems are not known by me or anyone else. Second, group members are independent human beings; one can go only so far in helping them solve their problems. A certain amount of good will and cooperation on the part of members is necessary for mutual problem solving; the leader cannot feasibly force members to cooperate. Third, some group process problems stem from what we have referred to earlier as individually oriented behaviors. There are things members do that are more closely related to their own personality dynamics than to group factors (i.e., showing off, dominating, bullying, avoiding work). Sometimes the group, with the help of the leader, can assist in resolving process problems caused by such behavior, and sometimes other measures (such as outside help) are required. A fourth risk in prescribing solutions to process issues has to do with *situational contingencies*. An approach that is useful in solving a problem under one set of circumstances will not work in others. For example, a suggestion for clarifying a garbled communication exchange between two people by asking another member to rephrase what she has heard each say may work well in a mature group, but less so in a new group in which defenses are high.

Our fifth and last reservation is the influence of the personal skill and style of the leader. As we all know, because of their rapport and trust with members, their sense of timing, or their intuition regarding members' feelings, some leaders can say nearly anything and make it a success. Others of us are less fortunate. We need the skill and self-confidence that comes from practice and feedback before a wise intervention has maximum impact.

In the face of all these caveats we shall, however, proceed with our guidelines for dealing with process issues.

COMMUNICATION

There are two major problems with group communication. One is that the exchange of ideas and feelings in an ongoing system is extremely complex and fraught with pitfalls. The other is that practically every process difficulty is labeled "a communication problem." I have sat with groups for hours, helping them review their operations and untangle a skein of dysfunctions ranging from lack of commitment to conflict over goals, only to have some sage lean back and pronounce, "I told you, it all boils down to poor communications." Thus, the first admonition for improving a group's communication is to be very sure that's what the problem is. Deep-seated subgroup rivalries, for example, will not go away just because members get their message across better to each other. Neither will a lecture on the virtues of two-way communication help a group make better decisions when it doesn't know how.

Groups suffer frustration and loss of performance due to communication problems when barriers of one sort or another keep the full *meaning* of a message from being transmitted from the mind of one person to the mind of another. The barriers may reside in the speaker (sender), in the group environment, or in the listener (receiver). The possibilities for error are almost infinite, and they have been the subject of extensive investigation. We will deal with the three areas separately in order to simplify our analysis.

Barriers in the Sender

Communication may be poor because of some things the sender (speaker) is doing or not doing. For example:

(a) *Poor presentation skills in speaking or discussing.* We all know some members who do not "get their ideas across" well. They stumble, repeat themselves, speak in endless phrases instead of sentences, can't be understood, don't know when to quit. We often turn them off, quit listening. The incapacities may stem from poor command of language or inability to organize thoughts and present them. Sadly some people whose performance in groups is important to their careers have struggled for years without fully recognizing the problem, or getting help with it. Supportive feedback, either inside or outside the group (depending on the climate and the member's resiliency), is the difficult first step, followed by appropriate training sessions. There are useful, learnable techniques for improving the quality of communication.

(b) *Emotional blocks to effective presentation.* A set of behaviors similar to those in (a) may stem from feeling tense, awkward, and on the spot when speaking in groups. At the knowledge level (command of the language and presentation), skills may be satisfactory until one is in the spotlight. Then, as one member put it, "my tongue becomes all thumbs." Under such conditions members often find it difficult to realistically evaluate their own input. They may speak too fast, too slow, too little, too much. Low self-confidence and fears of disconfirmation, often growing out of negative experiences in past interpersonal situations, may be the cause. There are several approaches to assisting members with this very common problem. The first steps, again, are acknowledgement of the problem and feedback. Often a mature group can be extremely helpful and supportive. In other cases, outside resources such as speaking classes or toastmasters' clubs may help by providing a support system of people with similar needs. A salient point is that discomfort in groups is nothing to be ashamed of; it stems from past experiences largely out of the individual's control (as do attitudes toward accordion music and taste for cauliflower).

(c) *Interference from peripheral cues.* Sometimes it is not the main message itself that causes trouble, but other information that is being transmitted simultaneously. One phenomenon that fits this category is *nonverbal* communication (facial expressions, physical postures, fidgeting), popularly called "body language." We all have a good deal of experience in reading nonverbal behavior, even though we are not always aware that we are doing so. For most of us, our practice began with the very important business of "psyching out" our parents to figure out how they were feeling. The problems with nonverbal behavior in groups are (a) that there may be *incongruence* between the content of what is being said and the meaning suggested by body language ("Your lips tell me 'no, no,' but there's 'yes, yes' in your eyes"), and (b) we are almost always left to *infer* the thoughts and feelings behind nonverbal behavior, and may be wrong in our inference. A member may assert great confidence in an idea but look doubtful, claim to be at ease but look tense and afraid, or express verbal support of another member but look antagonistic. Such mixed messages require guesswork to interpret and may confuse group communication. One reason for building a group climate that lowers defenses is to remove the need for members to protect themselves by talking differently from the way they feel.

Another technique is to call the member's attention to the incongruity, as you perceive it ("Joe, you say you agree with Mary's idea, but I can't help wondering if your tone of voice and the expression on your face don't suggest you have some reservations"). This is a sensitive intervention, however, because to suddenly be made aware that one's feelings are being observed via nonverbal behavior can be threatening and can increase defensiveness.

Barriers in the Group or Situation

There are a number of factors that can interfere with communication that have less to do with the sender or receiver than they do with conditions in the situation. Some of the more common of these follow.

(a) *Bad physical setting.* Good communication can be hampered by such obvious factors as poor acoustics, background noise, having people seated so that they cannot see each other talking, or too much physical distance between members (as on an assembly line). Many of these factors may be obvious and others may not be possible to change. It is useful to ask members if there are things in the situation that are hampering their communication.

(b) Another group level problem has to do with the *rules and procedures* that are used to run meetings and coordinate communication. Highly structured parliamentary procedures are intended to control discussion and to respond to the will of the majority with minimum time usage. They are usually not effective in small groups where the emphasis is on problem solving, developing effective working relations, and other ongoing tasks. Members tend to feel blocked and to lose their good ideas before they present them. They also are likely to switch from an interactive give-and-take discussion, which may build on itself, to a more strategic speech-giving style.

On the other hand, an effective group discussion approach is not totally without ground rules and organization. A set of mutual expectations, whether formal or informal, about such factors as an equitable distribution of discussion time, paying attention, not interrupting, and how consent and dissent are to be expressed is highly valuable. A discussion process that is too unstructured can be as frustrating to members as an overstructured one.

(c) *Leadership style and climate.* In the previous chapter we discussed leadership style and its effect on climate. Both of these factors also affect communication. Researchers have noted that some group leaders exert a high degree of control on communication by acting as the centralized "switchboard." All communications are channeled through them, and members must often address the leader rather than each other. Other leaders may, by their behavior, promote a highly formal and rational climate. Still others may engage in or encourage judgmental and evaluative behavior and contribute to a defensive climate. These climatic factors and the others we have discussed affect the amount of communication, the direction of its flow, its content, and its emotional tone.

(d) *Lack of interest or commitment.* When communication is sparse, flat, or seems to have a low level of energy, members may be demonstrating a lack of investment in what is taking place. The comment "We seem to be having communication problems" may constitute an attempt to find a cause that is easier to deal with than to have to say, "We really aren't motivated to work hard on this problem."

(e) *Differences and conflicts.* A major communication barrier in some groups for some people has to do with the threat and uncertainty of exposing one's values and viewpoints, which may be different from those of others. Groups that contain differences are likely to have difficulty communicating freely until they have worked out ways of discussing that lower the threat. One approach is to identify the differences (which may go unspoken for agonizingly long periods of time), bring them out into the open, and talk about how they can be dealt with with minimal heat.

Barriers within the Receiver

We turn now to a list of characteristics of those on the receiving end of communication that contribute to a message being missed or misunderstood.

(a) *Poor listening.* Effective listening is a combination of skills and attitudes. Although speaking skills get more attention, listening is equally important, if for no other reason than that sheer numbers dictate that we will spend more time listening than talking. Probably the first requisite for good listening is an attitude that values what other people in the group have to say, and anticipates gaining something from listening. (Individuals with over-grown egos who place little value on others are often poor listeners.) Another element is openness to hearing the other's message, the ability to say, "At this stage I just want to get as much information as I can about what the other person has to say without trying to change, counter, convince, or one-up her." A final element is called "active listening" and involves participating in the communication process by drawing the other person out, providing encouragement and support, asking clarifying questions, and assuming some of the responsibility for making an effective communication link.

(b) *Filtering the message.* One of the psychological characteristics of humans that protects us but also causes us problems is our tendency to screen out of our perception those things that are distasteful, threatening, or in conflict with our beliefs. In some cases psychological defenses are such that the bad news is blocked from our consciousness—we literally do not hear it. In other cases we hear it but discount it, ignore it, or explain it away. The leader should not be surprised if a significant piece of negative information is not immediately taken to heart by the group, but instead is misunderstood, reinterpreted, argued against, and rationalized. One way to cope with this communication barrier is to ask members to discuss how they feel about the information, rather than to continue reiterating the content.

(c) *Self talk.* Another common barrier to good listening is the tendency to rehearse in one's own head what one will say next, rather than listening to what is currently being said. Most of us carry on an ongoing dialogue with ourselves which involves evaluating our experiences and preparing for our next move. This tendency is common in defensive groups in which members must weigh carefully what they say, and in competitive groups in which members are trying to look good and outdo each other. A good clue to this barrier is a chain of events in which members' statements are not responses to the last speaker's input, but seem to be independent statements for different agendas. Many people are not aware that they and others are prone to this barrier; one helpful intervention is to describe our own tendency to rehearse internally and ask members if they also do it. Often they will find it a useful and amusing concept.

(d) *Resistance to influence.* As we have seen before, there are significant elements of power and control in groups, from both leaders and members. For some members who are concerned about being influenced, opening oneself to being communicated with fully may imply a risk of being unduly controlled. Thus one way to resist influence is to resist communication. Members who discount others' ideas and don't want to hear what colleagues have to say may be resisting control. It may be useful to point out that a person can listen fully and emphatically to what another has to say and still reserve the right to decide whether to agree.

These are only a few of the barriers to group communication. Each leader will collect his own additions. Probably the most helpful first steps are to begin building a norm that values good communication and to set aside time for the group to examine its communication effectiveness regularly.

COOPERATION VERSUS COMPETITION

In the chapter on values we pointed out the basic ambivalence most us have about whether we should compete or cooperate. We have received mixed messages from parents and other elements of society which say that the two modes of interaction are both desirable and undesirable. The same confusion carries into groups. We tell members, "We're all in this together," and then we run competitive contests. Or we stress democratic group decision making, but encourage members to "sell" their ideas and get credit for them. Sometimes groups are too cooperative and "groupy"; more frequently in Western societies group members compete (for visibility, credit, to win) when they should be cooperating.

Effective cooperation requires a degree of selflessness, the willingness to defer some immediate rewards for the greater good and a longer-term payoff. I am frequently asked to do a "team-building" session for a management group. Upon further investigation it usually turns out that the organization has unwittingly rigged the system to foster competition. Managers are forced to compete for budget dollars, positions, new equipment, and even for productivity prizes. It is then hoped that in one day a consultant can teach some principles or deliver some morals that will turn the group into a unified team. If members are offered rewards or incentives that will be differentially awarded on the basis of group-related behavior (inside or outside the group) they are highly likely to compete. If working together brings everyone greater rewards, they *may* cooperate. But because of prior socialization it is not unusual for members to engage in win/lose competition even when everyone could gain by cooperation.

Most leaders are good at identifying competitive behavior because they themselves are likely to have engaged in competition in order to gain their position. When difficulties or misunderstandings regarding cooperation and competition begin to arise, there are several things that can be done. The first is to develop with the group an understanding about what the two alternatives are, and which is needed in the present situation. The second step is to be clear about which behaviors the group and organization are encouraging by deeds and policies regardless of spoken aspirations. The advantages *to the members* of collaborative as opposed to competitive behavior need to be clearly drawn.

CONTROL

Control as a process issue refers to concerns and behaviors regarding competition for, and acceptance of, leadership. In groups in which the distribution of authority is well worked out and accepted there will probably be a minimum of control issues. Control problems are likely to raise their heads in groups in which the leaders' styles are ambiguous, the formal authority is disliked or distrusted, or members' agendas for the group are at odds.

Control problems exist when the group has trouble agreeing on how to decide what to do. There is, in such cases, the lack of a "guidance system" that will coordinate everyone in the group. If the formal leader issues a directive and members verbally or nonverbally resist, raise countless questions and objections, ignore the directive, intentionally misinterpret it or subvert it, there are probably control problems. Likewise, if in groups where leadership is shared, there is constant maneuvering, infighting and blocking among cliques or interest subgroups, there are control problems. If there are strong, assertive personalities who try to sway the group but find themselves blocked by others, the issues have to do with control. And if the leadership is at cross-purposes with the membership about how authority is exerted, the ensuing problems fall into the category of control.

There are several things that one may try in order to free a group from the frustration and disarray of control problems. A first step is to be as clear as possible about the origin, power, and style of the designated leadership. A second and related point is to work early in the group's life on those aspects of the psychological contract that have to do with leadership and control. Do members understand the authority system? Have they been given an opportunity to "contract" with the leadership by discussing mutual expectations, obligations, and prerogatives? Are members willing to accept the mode of control that the leaders propose? (Acceptance, in the contract sense, of a leadership/control system is a thornier problem than it first appears. Even in industrial situations in which individuals are hired and paid to obey commands, real acceptance is not automatic. There are countless ways of resisting control if there is no clear mutual contract.)

A third avenue to coping with control issues is to ensure that concerns and resistances related to the group's control processes are made legitimate and important topics for discussion. A group norm system that inhibits open discussion of control concerns (perhaps because authority is seen as non-negotiable) is a setup for problems. The insecure leader who expects his wishes to be followed quickly and automatically without discussion and possible disagreement is cutting off valuable sources of information.

A fourth mechanism for working out control problems is to hold individuals and subgroups clearly responsible for owning up to and resolving their differences in respect to group guidance. Elements of the group who are aware that their control contests are known about and understood are more likely to face the problem of resolving them. Contesting leaders and members need to consider and resolve the question of how a concerted group approach can be developed that will allow progress to be made while at the same time responding as much as is feasible to the varying agenda.

COMMITMENT

Commitment is one of the central membership issues in many groups and organizations. It most often refers to the degree to which members identify with the purposes, goals, and procedures of the group, accept the leadership, and expect to obtain rewards by co-operating. Lack of commitment means that members have not "bought into" the thrust of the group because they do not like or agree with it, or because they do not anticipate significant rewards for their willingness to give up short-term personal gains for group goals. Symptoms of lack of commitment include poor attendance, apathy, low energy, nonacceptance of or lack of enthusiasm about group goals, and unwillingness to accept responsibility. Groups with low commitment often operate at very superficial levels, discussing things insufficiently before deciding, settling for old ways of doing things rather than stretching for new ones, and deciding matters by majority vote rather than delving into basic issues.

When lack of commitment is of the kind described above, easy solutions such as pep talks and group picnics are unlikely to be of much help. Probably the best first step is a clarification of member desires, expectations and group goals. If the problem stems in part from misunderstanding, such clarification may help. For example, a task force of experts from various departments is often appointed to study a problem that cuts across the departments. The officer ap-pointing such a task force might neglect to explain clearly (a) what the problem is, (b) why the task force was appointed, (c) what is ex-pected of it, (d) what will happen to its report, and (e) what rewards, if any, members will receive for their participation. This is not an un-usual set of conditions, and leads to low commitment for reasons that now should be obvious. The solution begins with clarification by the appointing authority of the above questions and an emphasis on the importance of the assignments. Some organizations I have worked with go a step further by making performance on task forces and committees a significant component of the regular appraisal interview.

Another cause for low commitment that is different from those above stems from feelings of hopelessness or frustration. Members who belong to groups that have unreachable or unrealistic goals or lack the resources or expertise to accomplish their goals have diffi-culty identifying with the group because to do so means accepting the responsibility for failure. It is safer to remove oneself psycho-logically and say, in effect, "I don't care."

Both causes of low commitment can be viewed as problems with the psychological contract. If the leader expects members to be com-mitted, but members do not perceive reasons for commitment, the balance of rewards and costs must be re-evaluated.

CONFORMITY

As we mentioned in the second chapter, one of the classic dilemmas in groups is the tug and pull between individuality and conformity. The process issue related to conformity arises when the group evolves norms and standards for behavior and exerts pressure on members to adhere to them. Such a process is viewed by most scholars as a natural tendency. Tension rises in a group when a member deviates from accepted patterns. Members become concerned when the standard practices they have evolved for smooth functioning are violated. Even though they are not all written down as rules, every group develops a set of expectations about what is desirable. All one has to do to test this notion is to sit in a different chair from one's "normal" seat, argue with those who are the accepted experts, raise questions about the efficacy of long-standing procedures, or engage in humor when the group is serious. In all these cases, unless you are the leader, you are quite likely to feel pressure to "get back into line." Sometimes this pressure exerted by the group is direct, but often it is subtle.

Leavitt provides a rather chilling but realistic example of the stages a group goes through to pressure the deviant back into conformity.[1] In his example a member advocates an action that is in opposition to the views of the other members. First the others listen politely and pleasantly, hoping to seduce the wayward member into agreeing with them. Then they focus on the deviant, asking for further information. Then they try rational arguments. Next they suggest a reinterpretation, hoping the problem is a misunderstanding. When this fails, they point out that the deviant is holding up the group and suggest he "go along." The next strategies are ridicule followed by direct attacks on his competence and loyalty. Finally the group flatly rejects the deviant's ideas and rejects him along with them, engaging in "psychological amputation" of the troublesome person and behaving as though he is no longer even physically present. The deviant has had his membership taken away. Whether this is a healthy process or a rather sick one depends both on where you stand on the issue and how you feel (your values) about the individuality–conformity issue.

Without some willingness to compromise, to change one's mind sometimes and to go along for the common good, it would be difficult for most groups to get anything done. When everyone is locked into his or her position, things can be pretty well frozen. On the other hand, conformity and giving in for the sake of keeping the peace or in the interest of saving time can, in the long run, make for a dull and sterile group. There needs to be a balance.

Earlier we discussed Irving Janis's studies of classic cases in which conformity led to disastrous results. In his analyses of such groups as the National Security Council when it decided on the Bay of Pigs invasion, Janis identified the condition he called *groupthink.* In groups that are highly involved and cohesive, members may sacrifice their abilities to realistically appraise the situation in order to sustain unanimity. Under such conditions members may: (a) begin to feel potent and invulnerable and take too many risks, (b) rationalize away information that casts doubt on the validity of the group's stance, (c) believe they are more moral and right than others, (d) discourage the expression of dissident views from inside or outside the group, and (e) perceive that the group's views represent the preponderant and accepted viewpoint. Such behaviors may, of course, cause groups to make serious errors and to perform below the capacities of individual members. Overemphasis on maintaining a peaceful, cohesive, consensual group needs to be guarded against.

A related occurrence that is popular in the research literature is the *risky shift phenomenon.* This is the possibility that when individuals get together in groups to plan action, the group is likely to take more risks than would the individuals acting alone. The effects of such an event can be positive or negative, depending on the success or failure of the action taken.

There are no easy solutions to the individuality–conformity problem. It represents a basic dilemma in human behavior. A first step is for the leader to think through his or her own attitudes about conformity in groups. Are you a leader who feels more comfortable when things are fairly homogeneous and who tends to react negatively to differences? If so, your groups are likely to move in the direction of conformity and away from individuality of expression. A second step can be to stay on the lookout for over-conformity—members looking and acting like peas in a pod, no one disagreeing with the official position, keeping the peace at all cost. Third, if conformity becomes a problem the leader can reward constructively deviant behavior ("I appreciate hearing from you, Alice. I realize you're taking some heat for questioning the group's position, but this is an important issue and it's crucial that we hear all sides."). A fourth possibility is for the leader to "model" some degree of nonconformity to illustrate that wider ranges of behavior are possible and can be tolerated.

CONFLICT

> Were I to ask you to associate freely to the word "conflict," I predict I would receive three kinds of responses. One set of terms would have grisly and negative connotations—"war," "death," "destruction," "disorder," "aggressiveness," "violence," "rape." A second set of terms would have positive connotations—"adventure," "opportunity," "drama," "fun," "excitement," "development." A third set of terms would be relatively neutral, affectively speaking—"tension," "competition," "scarcity," "mediation," "bargaining," "reconciliation."[2]

To which category do you belong? Do you fit into more than one? This quotation illustrates one of the main reasons groups have trouble dealing with conflict. For many people conflict, especially face-to-face interpersonal conflict, is distasteful and unnerving. It awakens in us old reactions out of the past when we were chastised for fighting or were frightened by an argument between our parents. We will avoid open conflict at almost any cost, including putting up with a member's obnoxious behavior, going along with something we don't agree with, or biting our lip and upsetting our stomachs when we get angry.

Others of us may have quite different reactions. We may enjoy a good fight; we may be unconcerned about angry interactions and be in the habit of getting things off our chests and letting the chips fall where they may. Or we may be relatively unaffected by conflict, able to deal with it without much wear and tear but with no need to engage in it unless forced. In the typical organization the first style, avoidance of conflict, is usually most common. This approach is reinforced with the norms we have discussed before: The manager is always in control, doesn't display emotion, and resolves things by rational problem-solving techniques, not fights.

In most cases conflict that is ignored or avoided does not go away spontaneously. It becomes part of the fabric of the group and simmers below the surface, contaminating the group's process and occasionally bubbling up in uncontrolled episodes.

Conflict arises because of differences—in needs, goals, attitudes, values, and perceptions. And also because of competition for things of value—goods, wages, recognition, the feeling of winning, the triumph of an idea. Conflict arises also because we are emotional creatures who attach all sorts of feelings to events in our lives. A good healthy group conflict is not at all like two computers playing chess with each other. More is involved than logic and data. Egos go on the line, old reactions get stirred, adrenalin flows, strategies for winning and causing the other party to lose are initiated.

Conflict has been studied extensively and has been the subject of a variety of training approaches. Some useful tools for coping with it have emerged.

(a) Good planning can head off unnecessary conflict. Avoid arguments stemming from misunderstanding, inadequate information, or a bad psychological contract. Inform members fully about background information, goals, limitations, etc. Watch carefully for signs of inadequate information or misunderstanding and rectify them early. Also remember that competition can lead to conflict. Don't set it up by pitting one subgroup against another.

(b) Work to develop in the group the viewpoint that conflict is a natural and expected aspect of human interaction and that if it occurs it should be acknowledged, faced, and dealt with rather than avoided. This does not mean that shouting matches, personal insults, and win/lose battles need to be common occurrences. It does suggest that the leader should say, for example, "This discussion seems to be striking some sensitive nerves. Karl and Ted, you seem to be getting angry. Maybe we'd better see what's causing you to get upset before we try to solve the problem."

(c) When arguments do occur, try hard to get participants to own up to their feelings and deal with their own angers rather than casting aspersions on the other party. If a member can say, "*I* strongly disagree with Jerry, *I* don't like his idea at all and am getting very angry and upset," she is owning her feelings and her part in the disagreement. The member who says, "Jerry doesn't know what he's talking about! *He* ought to get his head out of the sand! *He's* messing up the group!" is disowning his feelings and blaming someone else for his anger. The notion that feelings are legitimate at all times but that we alone are responsible for our own feelings is a useful philosophy. Much unproductive conflict results from blaming others for emotions that reside solely within us.

(d) Strive to keep the disagreeing factions from getting locked into polarized win/lose positions. Once the battle lines are drawn and the opposing groups labeled it is harder to move into a problem-solving mode. Draw attention to similarities as well as differences, be aware of common goals, stress the importance of hearing and considering all points of view. Work toward *integrative* solutions in which the best aspects of all approaches are combined into an even better plan.

(e) Probably the most destructive form of conflict in groups and organizations is power politics, factions using covert and coercive tactics to win by "doing in" the opposition. The leader who plays power politics encourages others to do the same. In so far as the realities of the situation permit, keeping things straightforward and on top of the table turns out to be the best policy.

(f) Some conflict behavior in groups is not due to disagreements or power struggles about current issues. A member may start a fight with another because of an outside issue or because of what we referred to earlier as "personally oriented behavior." Although it makes sense to ask members not to bring their outside problems into the group, such control of feelings is often not possible. Neither is it the case that working groups should attempt to become therapy groups. However, a member whose behavior is highly troublesome to the others can damage collaboration unless dealt with. One approach for groups who do not have the services of a professional consultant is to deal directly and firmly with the *behavior* that is problematic without getting into underlying emotions, causes, or background factors. The troublesome member can be held responsible for doing what is necessary (including seeking outside help) to change to a less troublesome style.

In all these issues it is well to remember that the leader's own response to conflict has to be made a part of the equation. Are you comfortable enough with conflict to be able to deal with it without avoidance or over-reaction?

COHESIVENESS

We usually hope that the groups that are important to us will hold together as strong, close-knit, mutually supporting units. Some groups do, and some groups fall apart. The manager has a stake in doing what she can to encourage cohesiveness. In Likert's work on groups and organizations it was found that the highly productive units were cohesive. They had such characteristics as loyalty and attraction, acceptance of group values and goals, and supportive working relationships.[3] One group of authors refers to cohesiveness as ". . . the cement binding together group members and maintaining their relationships to one another."[4]

Although there are a variety of ways of analyzing cohesiveness in the social psychological literature, the major meaning is the degree of attraction the group holds for the individual and the resulting desire to remain in the group. This degree of attraction can stem from a number of factors, including a personal liking for and similarity to other members, acceptance of group goals and activities, and satisfaction with the leadership, decision-making process, structure, and climate. These factors are probably not absolute, but depend in part on the expectations about group membership and alternatives available to members.

The tools that the leader may use for building cohesiveness, then, have to do with increasing the members' attraction to the group. One strategy is to make sure members are compatible and reasonably similar in their views and styles. (When adding a new member to the group, some leaders give a major share of the choice to old members in order to enhance compatibility.) Another is to see that style of leadership and the various group procedures are as much to members' liking as circumstances allow.

Two less positive aspects of cohesiveness need to be mentioned. One is that a source of high cohesiveness for some groups is their strong mutual dislike of or opposition to another person or group. Some groups acquire cohesiveness as they unite to oppose a tyrannical leader. Others achieve such a state when they find themselves in conflict with another group. Using such dynamics intentionally to build cohesiveness has of course been done, but it is a tricky technique with possible unintended side effects such as an obsession to "do in" the other group.

It is possible for a group to become too cohesive to be effective. When members are highly dependent on one another for satisfaction and support and/or the resiliency of the system seems to be tenuous, there may be great reluctance to rock the boat by bringing up problems or unpleasant feelings. If this happens, concerns do not get dealt with, energy gets diverted into repressing conflict, productivity suffers, and members ultimately become dissatisfied (a problem in some families as well as other systems). Thus, sacrificing too much in order to gain cohesiveness may become self-defeating.

CONFIDENCE/TRUST

Trust is a basic ingredient in all human relationships, including groups. Most people who work with groups believe that in order for a collection of people to become a "real" group a degree of trust needs to develop. In order for communication to work well in a group a basis of trust must first be established. The same often holds true for the other positive process variables we have discussed, such as cooperation and commitment. Trust is an important element in the leadership climate models of Gibb and Argyris, which we discussed in the last chapter. If members do not trust each other enough to relax, to let down their guards a little, to risk a new idea, or to disclose a feeling, the group is likely to remain sterile and unrewarding.

Trust, however, cannot be created by the leader alone. You cannot build a trusting group out of untrustworthy people. Neither can you build a trusting group in an organization that sets members against each other in win/lose games; and you cannot create trust in highly political environments in which strategies are employed in the use of information. The best you can hope for is a set of agreements with regard to what is safe and what is unsafe.

In groups in which people desire to build trust and in which circumstances do not make openness too dangerous, higher levels of mutual trust and confidence are a possibility. Usually the development is a slow incremental process. One or more members take a risk (sometimes unintentionally) by doing something that exposes them to possible loss of esteem or makes them vulnerable to some manipulation. If the group supports the risk-taker, valuing and reinforcing the behavior, the trust potential goes up and increases the possibility that another member will risk. For example, a member of a new group might feel tense and apprehensive about the uncertainty of working with strangers. Instead of maintaining silence and trying to look cool, she might decide to risk sharing her feelings with the others. (Some people, for example, find doing so frees them from much of the tension.) If the group makes light of the member's expressed concerns, tells her "You shouldn't feel that way," or teases her, she is unlikely to take such a risk again, as are other members. On the other hand, if the others show concern, own up to some of the same feelings themselves, and discuss how to overcome such feelings of beginning awkwardness, the trust level will begin to build and members will feel enough confidence in each other to risk the expression of other concerns: "I don't understand our mission," "I need some help with my assignment," "I have a far-out idea I'd like to try out on you all!"

Giffin and Barnes have identified several factors that commonly contribute to the development of interpersonal trust.[5] Three personal characteristics of persons who engender trust in others emerge in a number of studies. These are *expertness*, *reliability*, and *dynamism*. Expertness involves the perception that the trusted individual has appropriate skill, knowledge, or other competency to deserve one's faith. Reliability, the most important factor in several studies, involves the perception that the person is dependable, moral, sincere, and of good will. Dynamism refers to a collection of such characteristics as assertiveness, decisiveness, openness, and frankness.

In group situations there are additional factors that affect the development of trust. Many resolve around the judgment of whether potential gains from trust building outweigh possible losses (an *expectancy* phenomenon). Thus, we weigh the possibility that the other person will violate our trust (use something we say against us, for example). And we also ask ourselves whether promises of trust can be checked on and enforced.

CLOSENESS/INTIMACY

A concern in many groups, especially full-time groups such as work units (as opposed to committees which meet once a month) is how close members will become. Will they form warm friendships, discuss personal lives and problems, socialize outside of work? Or will they maintain more distant, formal, and business-oriented relationships? Interpersonal closeness in a work setting is a two-edged sword. Many people feel that the workplace should not be dehumanizing, that it should not require that working relationships be sterile, power oriented and non-nurturing. They believe that some of the problems of our contemporary industrial society, such as alienation, game playing and stereotyping, are heightened by our tendency to depersonalize work relationships. On the other hand, there is evidence that working groups that develop too high a level of friendship and rapport can become ineffective. They are likely to avoid facing conflict, making tough decisions, and dealing with differences because they do not want to jeopardize the warmth and support they receive from the group.[6] The leader, then, may find it necessary to determine the upper and lower limits of closeness that are compatible with the group's goal.

Those who have worked extensively with training groups have been struck by the frequency with which members express needs for close-knit, supportive relationships. When the group has achieved a level of trust that makes such expression possible, there seems to be a latent desire, and thus the potential, for intimacy among many people. On the other hand, some members may feel quite differently. They may prefer more distant and formal interactions, perhaps because they were socialized to dislike or fear too much closeness with non-family members or because their needs for such interaction are fully met in other situations. These different preferences for closeness can become a problem for the groups. If the leader becomes aware that there are conflicting pressures with regard to closeness versus distance it may be useful to bring the issue into the open for discussion. Often those who are seeking more intimacy will feel they are being deprived of something they need by the more impersonal members. Those who prefer distance are likely to feel they are being pressured or crowded. It may happen that each subgroup has an exaggerated view of what the other wants, and clarification of expectations will allow a middle ground to be reached. It may also happen that the group as a whole will have to make some choices that will not satisfy everyone. A possibility is that there can be some differential treatment—a member may contract to remain emotionally distant from an otherwise intimate group (not an easy arrangement).

So far, this discussion has deliberately stayed away from those aspects of intimacy that involve romantic or sexual relationships. Needless to say, that topic raises a different set of issues. We all know that sexual attraction is a possible outcome of close working relationships among mixed-sex groups or sometimes among the same sex.

What we may be less clear about is that there can be sexually related feelings in many of the dynamics of groups, for example, attraction, rivarly, jealousy, intimidation, and protectiveness. Although in many working groups there are taboos against recognizing and expressing sexual issues, that does not stop the feelings or their impact on the group's work. In counterpoint to the taboos are occasional concerns that women and men working together will be overcome by passion and lose control of themselves. As two women authors on management point out, such ideas are myths that may be used as excuses.[7]

It is risky to attempt to give the leader advice about how to deal with sexual issues in working groups. Values are changing, we are just beginning to come out of a period of stereotyping and biases, and the research on sexual relations in work is sparse and inconclusive. Management folklore about separating work and sex is probably fairly well founded and is as good as anything we presently have to go on. Intimate relationships set those involved off from the others, create the potential for conflict and inauthenticity, and bring up emotional issues that most managers are not equipped to deal with. Among the things the leader can do are: (a) establish a clear contract or expectations about the limits of sexual relations among members, (b) be sensitive to possible emotional issues stemming from sexual attractions (jealousy, protectiveness, competiton, etc.), (c) treat sex-related issues that do occur as special cases of human relationship problems that need to be faced and dealt with, rather than as taboos to avoid, and (d) avoid all expressions of sexism that serve to distort relationship problems and make them more difficult to deal with.

COMPETENCE

One of the most underrated and unresearched process issues has to do with differences in the competence levels among members and how the differences are dealt with. It is relatively easy to say, "Sarah, you and Joe seem to be having trouble communicating with each other. Why don't you rephrase what he just said?" It is not at all easy to say, "Joe, your lack of knowledge about the topic and your ineptness in participating in the problem solving are slowing down the group and making us lose efficiency. Why don't you drop out for a while?"

My experience is that most members have difficulty dealing with their perception that another member is significantly less able to perform intellectually or emotionally. While we all recall the unrelenting professor who flunked the nice but marginal student without a qualm and the tough-minded executive who fired every employee who made a mistake, such types are the exception. For whatever reason, most of us have trouble dealing directly and incisively with incompetence, including incompetence among group members. One of the problems is that lack of competence is usually not a problem that can be "worked through." That is, a healthy and open discussion will not cause it to go away.

My guess is that groups are stymied more frequently than we realize because a less competent member is being protected rather than being dealt with. Not that problems of incompetent performance should always be surfaced and discussed. Too many personal and situational factors need to be considered. It is, however, a suggestion to the leader to be on the lookout for process problems caused by incompetence. If facing and discussing such issues within the group is not feasible, perhaps an external solution such as more training, transfer to another group, or coaching would be in order.

CHANGE

"Response to Change" would be a more descriptive title for this section. Ironically, many groups are developed to create and bring about change. But especially after they have been functioning for a while, they may become resistant to change. The generalization "employees resist change" is often stated in the management literature. Research on this assumption has produced mixed results, but tends to support the notion that resistance to change is not a basic human trait. People resist change when they feel threatened or confused by it, when they believe they will be outmoded, when harder or faster work will be required, when social groups will be broken up, when one will be replaced, or when one's ideas or projects will no longer be valued.

There is an extensive literature on the planning of change, including such topics as organization development and change agent roles. The reader who is encountering serious problems in implementing change is encouraged to conduct further research on the subject.[8] In this section we will only sketch some of the highlights of the field.

Resistance to change should be suspected when each new idea is beaten down with reasons why it can't be done; when programs to do something new die without being implemented; when new projects are killed by intentional neglect or by sabotage; when suggestions for improvements are not actively rejected, but are talked to death or relegated to a subcommittee. It should be noted that there are occasions when what looks like resistance to change has very little to do with the proposed change itself, but stems from one of the other process issues, such as hostility toward the leader, conflict among subgroups, low trust, and so on. In such cases, the resistance to change is a symptom rather than a cause. If, however, it is the *change itself* that is being resisted, the leader can proceed with some of the suggestions that follow.

The first suggestion for engendering a more positive response to change is to communicate with members as early and fully as possible about upcoming changes. Rumors, apprehensions, and loss of trust stemming from changes that are sprung on groups are a common and often unnecessary cause of resistance. Second, there is ample evidence that members are much less resistant when they participate in planning and implementing change. Participative approaches to change more fully utilize member resources, build a greater sense of ownership, and allow members to feel a measure of control over the change process. A third suggestion is to diagnose the sources of resistance as well as the factors acting to encourage change. The *force-field analysis* derived from the work of Kurt Lewin is a commonly used tool for such a diagnosis.[9] Lewin's assumption was that a given situation is held in a state of equilibrium (nonchange) because the forces acting to bring about change (the driving forces) are counteracted by the forces acting to restrain the change. By involving the group in listing and weighing both sets of counter-forces and developing strategies for overcoming the restraining forces, the leader may be able to get the change process moving.* A fourth suggestion is to strive to increase the group's readiness for change (change strategists use the term "unfreezing"). Groups that continually monitor and evaluate their own internal processes as well as their effectiveness in respond-

---

*See Item 4 in the Learning Aids section at the end of this chapter.

ing to external demands are more amenable to change than those that assume they will continue to operate in a stable state.

CLIMATE

The climate or atmosphere or emotional tone of a group is a somewhat subjective, but nevertheless significant factor. You can spend an hour with a group and feel fairly confident in rating it on several climate-related dimensions: tense versus relaxed, warm versus cold, open versus closed, happy versus glum, friendly versus unfriendly, etc. In the chapter on leadership we cited the work of Gibb and Argyris on group climate as it related to leadership behavior. They emphasize the degree of support and acceptance provided to members, as opposed to a punitive or defense-producing climate.

Group climate is usually a dependent variable, that is it depends on, or is a result of, other factors and process issues. A group may be tense and distant because that is the climate of the overall organization to which they belong, or because the leader is tense and cold and discourages warmth, or because there is a high degree of win/lose competiton going on between two subgroups, or for many other reasons. The value of considering climate as a separate process issue is that members can, with some help, readily get in touch with the climate and its impact on them. They can also evaluate the climate and whether they want to try to change it. It is possible, for example, that some climate factors have become habitual but have never really been openly evaluated. A group may find itself operating in a very formal, standoffish, and nonsupportive fashion and decide it wants to work on ways to modify that stance. It can consider easing some of the procedures and formalities, getting to know each other better, and identifying sources of unnecessary competition.

There are several possibilities for identifying the climate of a group. One is simply to reflect one's perception of the climate and ask others to share theirs. ("As we work together I get the feeling that this group is fairly reserved and cool and reluctant to speak out. How do the rest of you feel about the 'climate'?") Another is to pass out slips of paper and ask members to write down anonymously three or four objectives that describe the way the group feels to them. These can then be collected, written on a blackboard, and discussed. Still another approach is to ask one member to observe the group as it operates, to rate it according to several climate variables, and then to lead a discussion about the climate.

CONCLUSION

The list of 12 process issues we have discussed is only one way of cutting the pie. There are other lists and other ways of describing what goes on as people work together. Furthermore, there is not always a clean separation between the categories. In a given situation they may overlap and blend together, or even form cause–effect relationships with each other. Nevertheless, the leader who learns to identify these issues will have a useful schema for improving working relationships in groups. It is true, of course, that identifying and understanding problems does not mean they are automatically solved. But it means that the first stages of problem solving have begun.

LEARNING AIDS

1. For each of the process issues listed below, see if you can think of an example of how that issue occurs in one of your target groups. If feasible, check your perception with one or more members of the group.
   A. Communication
   B. Cooperation versus competition
   C. Control
   D. Commitment
   E. Conformity
   F. Conflict
   G. Cohesiveness
   H. Confidence/trust
   I. Closeness/intimacy
   J. Competence
   K. Change
   L. Climate
2. Select one of the issues to discuss with members of the group. Plan a strategy for introducing the discussion so as to minimize threat and resistance. Test your proposed intervention on another member of the group before introducing it.

3. Look again at the list of 12 process issues. Which do you feel most comfortable with and capable of handling? Which do you feel most uncomfortable with and least capable of handling? What steps can you take to improve your performance in these areas?

4. Select a change problem that currently exists or is anticipated in one of your groups.
   A. Do a force-field analysis below by listing the factors that operate to bring about change (driving forces) and those that are inhibiting change.

Force-Field Analysis

Driving forces   Inhibiting forces

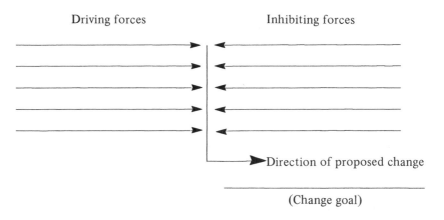

Direction of proposed change

(Change goal)

   B. Identify one or two of the inhibiting forces that seem to be strongest, and develop a plan for reducing or eliminating them.

NOTES

1. H. J. Leavitt, *Managerial Psychology* (Chicago: University of Chicago Press, 1978), p. 213.
2. This material is taken from Cyril R. Mill and Lawrence Porter (eds.), *Reading Book* (Washington, D.C.: NTL Institute for Applied Behavioral Science, 1982), p. 41.

3. Rensis Likert, *New Patterns in Management* (New York: McGraw-Hill, 1961).

4. Stanley Schachter, N. Ellertson, D. McBride, and D. Gregory, "An Experimental Study of Cohesiveness and Productivity" in *Group Dynamics: Research and Theory*, 3d ed., D. Cartwright and A. Zander, eds. (New York: Harper and Row, 1968).

5. Kim Giffin and Richard E. Barnes, *Trusting Me, Trusting You* (Columbus, OH: Charles E. Merrill Publishing, 1976).

6. S. D. Deep, B. Bass, and J. A. Vaughn, "Some Effects on Business Gaming of Previous Quasi-T-Group Affiliations," *Journal of Applied Psychology* \51 (1967): 426–31.

7. Rosalind Loring and Theodora Wells, *Breakthrough: Women into Management* (New York: Van Nostrand, Reinhold, 1972), Chapter 5.

8. W. G. Bennis, K. D. Benne, and R. Chin, *The Planning of Change* (New York: Holt, Rinehart and Winston, 1976).

9. Kurt Lewin, *Field Theory in Social Research* (New York: Harper & Row, 1951).

7

PROBLEM SOLVING GROUPS

The heads of the branch's six divisions reported to Executive Vice-President Al Dowling. Al liked to view the group as the "management team" and to involve them in discussion of company business, especially as it related to issues that cut across the divisions. The group met regularly for a couple of hours a week, and also came together on an ad hoc basis when problems arose. Discussion was usually relaxed and free flowing, as information was shared and ideas kicked around. In the past Al had made most of the final decisions, after having heard everyone's ideas. It was not uncommon for his decisions to be heavily influenced, or even changed, by the persuasive arguments of his experienced division heads.

The setting this morning, however, was somewhat different. The company's financial condition had deteriorated over the past several months. Sales were down because of increasing competition, and the organization needed cash to purchase new equipment to meet the competition. A stringent cost-cutting effort was to be undertaken. Al had received a dollar amount for the cut from corporate headquarters and was told to develop a cost-cutting plan that would minimize negative impact on productivity and morale. He decided that such a solution required the best possible information and judgment from all his division heads. He asked them to block out a full afternoon for an emergency meeting and when they assembled, he announced, "Here's the amount the branch has to cut. Since it's a problem that affects all of us, it will be a mutual decision. We'll meet until we come to agreement."

As the discussion began Al wished he had paid more attention to helping the group develop its problem-solving ability. The discussion would wander aimlessly for hours and deteriorate into a competitive battle with each member protecting his or her own turf. Al was painfully aware that the group needed a format for attacking the problem and skills in problem solving.

Finally, after six chapters about history, culture, and process it is time to tackle the topic that interests us most—effective problem solving. How can groups do a good job of what they're established for? How can the manager help them function effectively in dealing with and solving problems in a timely fashion? It's true, of course, that the topics we've covered thus far in this book do bear directly on effectiveness. You can't expect to take a group that is rent with internal competition, divided by lack of trust, unable to communicate, and confused about its leadership and turn it into an effective problem-solving mechanism simply by teaching it a set of fancy techniques. Process does have to do with effectiveness. And (sorry!) there are no short cuts. The first step in developing problem-solving effectiveness is to work through the issues discussed in the previous chapters. A common frustration for those who consult with groups is to be called in when the "fat is in the fire" (as in the Al Dowling case above) and be expected to overcome years of bad history in a one-day session. The best one can do, with luck, is to put on enough bandaids to help the group limp through its crisis. Rensis Likert, in his pioneering studies, found that members of highly effective groups are ". . . skilled in all the various leadership and membership roles and functions required for interaction between leaders and members and between members and other members."[1]

TASK COMPETENCE

It is true, of course, that effective problem solving requires subject matter expertise and task competence as well as process skills and a healthy climate. Thus a first question is, "Do we have the appropriate human resources to solve the problem? Do the members have the substantive background information, skills, and perspective to deal with the problem? The importance of this principle is self-evident, but it is violated frequently. The leader may fail to make an accurate assessment of the competencies needed, or the group may not want to admit its gaps. Often, in my experience, group members fear admitting they don't have the knowledge necessary, and thus they muddle through when a simple request for information at the beginning would have saved a great deal of time. In an in-basket training exercise I once ran, the participants received ambiguous and incomplete information about a major project they were expected to untangle. Only about one out of ten managers went back to their boss to say, "I need more information before I can deal with this project efficiently."

TWO PATHS TO PROBLEM SOLVING

An important dilemma in group problem solving, as in other areas of management, has to do with the trade offs between control-oriented rational techniques and a more organic, facilitative approach. Rational approaches to problem-solving usually require a disciplined adherence to a series of steps. A simplified model for such techniques might be:

1. Identify the problems
2. Define the desired outcome
3. Identify alternative solutions
4. Evaluate the alternatives according to relevant criteria (cost, time, probability of success, etc.)
5. Select the best alternative

This approach makes rational sense. It avoids the common pitfall of leaping to solutions before the problem is adequately defined and it forces the consideration of more than the first proposed alternatives. It is an application of the scientific method and has worked well in situations in which the problem can be defined in fairly clear-cut terms and where objective data are available. For example, if the problem is one of how and where to invest cash reserves on a short-term basis, the standard problem model makes good sense. Alternatives can be identified, objective data on interest rates can be utilized, decision makers can pool their knowledge of historical factors, trends, and risks, and a relatively objective selection can be made. The hitch is that the rational model is often not used, even in situations in which it fits the problem. This may be because of lack of knowledge of the technique, but there are other reasons. These include the fact that many people do not like to be tied to a rather rigid technique and also that the rational model is not very helpful with many "real" organizational problems. It is to this possibility that we turn next.

The more common organizational situation is one in which (a) there are signs that things are not going well, but there is no agreement about what the problem is, (b) data are subjective, contradictory, and hard to get, (c) vested interests, pride, and hidden agendas are present, (d) a solid solution will probably require some risks and changes in behavior, (e) the situation is liable to be impacted by unforseen events, and (f) it will be a while before it is possible to tell whether the solution works. Under these conditions the rational decision approach probably does not fit very well. Instead, a more open and synergistic process, but one that requires at least as much rigor as the rational model, is required. There is no single scheme that contains all the elements that I believe are necessary. The following approach combines important principles from several authorities.

WORKING THE PROBLEM

A term more apt than problem solving is *working the problem.*[2] After all, most real problems do not have a single elegant solution nor is there one right path to take. Working the problem connotes coming to grips with the problem the best one can, grappling with it with all the tools available, and sticking with it until a solution is implemented and tested. This broader view of problem solving can be divided into the following stages (which may overlap or even change sequence from one situation to another):

Building a climate for problem solving
Problem sensing/problem finding
Clarification
Testing members' reaction to the problem
Identification of necessary resources
Categorizing the problem
Sharing information and feelings
Looking out for pitfalls
Moving from divergence to convergence

The decision
Feasibility testing
Planning for follow-through
Reviewing/evaluating the process

Building a Climate for Problem Solving

To repeat a point made previously (one well worth repeating), good problem solving begins before a problem comes along. If the manager expects the group to solve problems when they arise, it is important to develop the group's capacity to function. Are the early-stage identity and trusts concerns resolved? Do members communicate well? Is the leadership process understood? Are problem-solving skills developed?

Problem Sensing/Problem Finding

If one hopes to solve a problem, the first step is to find it. If that statement sounds flippant, let it be understood that many significant group and organizational problems go unidentified or avoided until it is too late to deal with them in a reasoned way. Groups need to review information from inside and outside the group to see where things are beginning to slip, where once satisfactory solutions don't work so well any more, where conditions are changing, and/or where others keep assuring us, "Don't worry, there's no problem, this is just a temporary setback."

Edgar Shein has proposed an *adaptive coping cycle*, a series of steps whereby an organization may cope successfully with its environment.[3] The first stage is "sensing a change in some part of the internal or external environment." The second is, "importing the relevant information about the change into those parts of the organization that can act upon it, and digesting the implications of that information."

Leavitt uses the term *problem finding*.[4] This is the front-end, subjective phase of problem solving. It is the creative phase. At this stage choices determine long-term outcomes. Does the group identify and begin to work on the crucial issues for the organization's health, or does it simply content itself with safe little problems that are handed to it, "rearranging the deck chairs on the Titanic," oblivious to the more significant issues? There are plenty of barriers to problem finding. It often causes discomfort when a group begins to dig to look for questions. Management by exception (dealing only with things that are causing trouble) and "if it ain't broke don't fix it" are sentiments counter to problem finding.

Most groups can profit from an occasional session in which, without agenda, they ask, "What questions should we be asking?" "Are there problems we haven't confronted?"

Clarification

Once the problem is on the table, whether found by the group or handed to it by someone else, it needs to be thoroughly examined before searching for solutions. Is the problem clearly defined and understood to everyone's satisfaction? Is there common agreement about its definition? Many a group has experienced the wasted time that results when members have different perceptions of the problem.

A group I worked with met to discuss a complex problem. After the discussion ran on for a frustratingly long time without apparent progress, I asked them what the goal of the meeting was. One member implied that that was a rather naive question, they all knew perfectly well what the goal was. As that member stated the goal, for my benefit, others chimed in to say that that wasn't quite their understanding. It developed (much to the inner relief of the consultant) that there were as many perceptions of the goal as there were members. The discussion that followed served to develop a shared view of the problem to be worked on and helped unblock the discussion.

Testing Members' Reaction to the Problem

In some situations it is important to find out how the problem, once identified, causes members to feel. Do they find it interesting? Will they be motivated to devote energy to working through to a solution? Do they find it overwhelming? Will it realistically take so long to resolve that people will drop out? Is it too risky? There are many settings, of course, in which the group has little choice but to tackle the problem, if its consequence are significant. But lack of motivation to work on the problem is a common cause for poor group performance. It is far better to have any reservations or low commitment out on the table in the beginning, where they can be resolved, than to find them operating insidiously half-way through the process.

If there are more problems to be worked than there is time available for, certainly the degree of attraction to members should be an important criterion in the selection. Also, it may be possible to modify the problem statement to make it more acceptable (narrow it, broaden it, etc.).

Identification of Necessary Resources

As we indicated earlier, lack of sufficient resources (skills, information, equipment, funds) is another cause of low motivation and poor performance. The leader can usefully help the group to ask, "As we begin this process, do we have the right people in the room? Is the necessary expertise available? Do we need information that has not been provided us?"

While it is certainly true that seemingly there is never enough information, time, or money to do a really adequate job of dealing with a problem, there is a danger that the group will settle for an inferior solution if it does not clearly face the question of the adequacy of its resources. If pride, fear, or insensitivity to needs prevent a realistic assessment of resource requirements, the group may be operating with a serious handicap.

Categorizing the Problem/Determining the Method

You should not be surprised to find that no method works for all problems. Before beginning to work, it is well to ask, "What kind of problem is this, and what approach will be most useful?" Following is a list of some of the major kinds of problems groups deal with:

• *Exploration/understanding/finding out what's going on.* Example: The management committee meets weekly to assess how things are going in the plant. Members report on their functions and data from the management information system is shared. The problem is to understand as fully as possible the full range of performance factors and to identify those that need attention. The best method is an orderly progression through the reports with plenty of time for questions, clarification, inferences.

• *Evaluating alternatives—the classic decision-making model.* Example: The machine in the stamping department is breaking down frequently. A decision needs to be made whether to give the machine a major overhaul or replace it, and if it is replaced, which of several available new machines should be selected. A specification of each alternative is needed, along with relevant data, such as price, cost of operation, output, etc. A rational decision will select the alternative with the best cost/benefit picture, unless other variables (such as the company's cash-flow picture) are to be considered, or "nonrational" factors (such as the foreman's complaint that all the other departments got new machines) enter the picture.

• *Creating/coming up with a new idea.* Example: The company picnic is losing its appeal. Last year it was not well attended and this year is liable to be a total flop. A fresh new idea for an employee "event" is needed to give families a chance to get acquainted and to lower some of the hierarchical barriers. Brainstorming (tossing out ideas without evaluating them) may be a good place to start.

• *Resolving conflict.* Example: The parents' association and the school board are in opposition about whether to cut the athletic budget. Each group accuses the other of dubious motives and there is little communication. A meeting has been called to attempt to resolve the conflict. Those who feel a strong need to keep things cool and rational and decide everything on the basis of "fact" are likely to be uncomfortable in such a situation. Two respected authors state, "Almost the last thing you should do in analyzing a problem is to get the facts."[5] This statement, while a little tongue-in-cheek, pinpoints the difficulty with "facts." Whose facts? Why selected? Pertinent to what? What are facts to me may be seen as fabrications by you.

The technology of conflict management suggests the following steps: (a) Try to establish a process whereby each side can state fully its views and concerns and be listened to by the other side; (b) seek superordinate goals that both sides find highly desirable (such as providing our children the best college preparation available in the city);

(c) look for items that both groups can agree to; (d) try to ease the elements of conflict that do not have directly to do with substantive issues, for example, distrust, stereotyping, fear; (e) try to isolate the hard-core substantive issues and attempt to resolve them through creative problem solving, compromise, or negotiation.

• *Finding the cause(s) of undesirable situations.* Example: The symptoms are mounting that something is wrong in the legal department. Turnover is at an all-time high and response time on inquiries is causing complaints. The director of the unit asserts that nothing is wrong, she just ended up with some bad apples, which she plans to remove. The chief executive officer is concerned, and sets up an inter-departmental committee to look into matters and report their findings. The problem is one of diagnosis, and of coping with the probable defensiveness of the department head. The committee's methods will include data gathering (probably confidential) and analysis. The choice of final solution will be up to someone else.

• *Learning/generating information.* Example: Word-processing technology is developing at such a rapid rate that it is difficult for operating managers to keep up with the knowledge. The head of the information center organized a breakfast group that meets once a month to update each other. The problem is to share information in an efficient but interesting manner and to allow for a free exchange of questions and answers.

• *Creating rules, policies, structures.* Example: The steering committee of the metropolitan children's agency is a purely policy-making body. It does not get involved in operations or staffing. The organization's executive director brings to the committee's attention broad issues and recommendations for policy changes. The problem is to develop policies that resolve the issues without unintended side effects. A further problem is that policies developed by a citizen group outside the organization, with no employee involvement, often are not well understood and poorly implemented.

• *Catharsis.* Example: Nurses on the trauma ward deal daily with medical crises and human suffering. Their jobs are stressful and often subject them to strong emotions of sadness and frustration. Those on duty during each shift often gather informally at the nurses' station to share feelings, provide support, and help each other cope with the stress they are subjected to. The problem is to provide a group atmosphere that will help them maintain equilibrium in a difficult situation.

• *Building group morale, cohesivenss, and loyalty.* Example: The southeastern sales division consists of 16 saleswomen and salesmen who spend most of their time covering their regions. The product lines are complex and undergo constant change due to developing technologies. Because some customers have facilities in several regions, the salespeople frequently need to cooperate with each other. The divisional sales manager has found it helpful to call the sales force together on a bi-monthly basis not only to provide product information but to develop them as a team, with a sense of mutual responsibility and identification with the company. Otherwise they begin to operate like autonomous agents, to the detriment of the division. The problem is to build a team among individuals who function interdependently. (Team building as a group technology will be discussed in the next chapter.)

It should be evident that each of these kinds of problems (and this list is incomplete) requires a somewhat different approach. The manager who attempts to use *Robert's Rules of Order*, or the rational problem-solving model, or any other approach for all problems will be making a mistake. Problems in which creative generation of ideas is the most important element call for a tack quite different from a heated conflict or the evaluation of complex alternatives. Once this distinction is made in a given situation it is time to begin facilitating a useful discussion.

Sharing Information and Feelings

If you have determined that the problem to be solved can be best dealt with by a group (as opposed to one or more individuals working independently) then it is the quality of the group discussion that will make the difference between a good or a poor group output.[6] Here the skills of the manager as facilitator come into full play. Members should be encouraged to share freely their ideas and reactions They should understand clearly what is expected of them, how much time is available, how the final decision will be made, what the consequences of failure are. Quiet members should be encouraged, over-talkative ones gently quieted ("We've heard Al's ideas, now let's hear from Trudy."). A delicate balance is to exert some reasonable direction over the discussion without making members feel inhibited. (One manager told his group, "I want you to give me all your good ideas, not the silly ones, but the *good* ones!" Members used up most of their energy trying to be sure they didn't risk giving a silly idea.)

Looking Out for Pitfalls in the Process

As the discussion progresses it is well to remind oneself of the things that can occur to hamper the effectiveness of the problem-solving process. The following have been discussed previously, and will be repeated here as a reminder.

● *Hidden agendas.* Do members have goals, special interests, "axes to grind," which they are keeping covert, but which are influencing their participation?

● *Advocacy.* Open, objective problem solving suffers when some members advocate and push a certain alternative. Such a discussion may become more political than objective, and the effectiveness of the process suffers.

● *Personally oriented behaviors.* Cousins to hidden agendas are member behaviors that are based on internal personal needs, rather than group goals. These include posturing, bickering, one-up manship, and chauvinism.

● *Competitiveness.* If certain outcomes may be more favorable to some groups or individuals than to others, it is safe to anticipate some competition and therefore some bias in how information is perceived and weighed.

Moving from Divergence to Convergence

Some individuals are "divergent" in their thinking. That is, they tend to move in the direction of additional ideas, more alternatives, different ways of looking at things. Others are "convergers"; they seek to narrow the possibilities, pull things together, arrive at closure.[7] Groups also may be divergent or convergent in their discussion. In the earlier stages of problem solving, divergence is usually appropriate. It is important to generate as much information as possible, to keep the discussion open to more possibilities, to avoid jumping to conclusions. As the discussion progresses, however, after all the information and ideas are on the table, the time comes to move to convergence, pull things together, and arrive at decisions. The alert leader senses when the divergent phase of the discussion has gone on as long as is useful, and when it is time to move to convergence. "We seem to have covered all the information relevant to the problem, now we need to begin arriving at a decision," is one way to steer the discussion.

It should be noted that some groups stay in a divergence mode in order to avoid (consciously or unconsciously) having to make a decision. Especially if the decision is difficult to live with, creates more work, or causes some members to lose, there is a tendency to delay it with talk. There is always one more bit of pertinent information, another slightly different way of looking at things, someone who needs to be heard. If the group cannot seem to give up its divergent behavior, the leader may assist by asking the group to take a look at the way it is functioning.

The Decision

At some point the time arrives when the decision is to be made, the alternative selected, the avenue chosen that will (hopefully) solve the problem. It is very helpful to have specified well ahead of that time the decision-making mechanism that will be used. There are several available.

• *Consensus.* Because of its often positive effect on group morale, commitment, and follow-through, consensus has a good deal of appeal. Contrary to some popular opinion, consensus does not mean unanimity. Not everyone has to totally agree nor be perfectly satisfied with the outcome. Consensus is a process, a way of operating, and a philosophy. Consensus is achieved when every member can say, "I have had an opportunity to express my views fully, and they have been thoughtfully considered by the group. Even though this solution is not the one I believe is optimal it is acceptable and I will support it. I endorse the validity of the process we have undertaken." The leader plays an active role, but does not mandate the decision. Consensus is often not easy to achieve, and it can be time consuming and frustrating. It requires experience and commitment on the part of the group; but it has definite benefits.

• *Leader decides.* In many situations where the leader is "boss," the procedure is to talk the situation over with the members, listen to their suggestions and requests, and then to render a decision. This "consultive" approach is legitimate in group problem solving if certain concerns are kept in mind. One of the most common complaints I hear from group members is about the "phoney" group decision-making meeting. The leader calls the group together to solve a problem. After expending a good deal of effort, members finally realize that the leader's mind was made up before the group was called together. The meeting was a sham! The leader only wanted to create an illusion of participation, or perhaps to validate and gain support for a decision already made. Members become very adept at seeing through such a ruse. Needless to say they quickly lose their motivation and commitment.

If the leader wants only consultation before making a unilateral decision, the ground rules should be made perfectly clear at the outset. It helps if the leader indicates that the group will have a good deal of influence on the decision (if, indeed, it will) and that the pooled insights of members are expected to improve the quality of decision. A difficult aspect of the unilateral decision-making approach is the "macho temptation." In some circles it is clearly the norm that any leader worth *his* salt doesn't lean on the group, but stands up like a man, makes his own decisions, and deals with the consequences. While this approach may be appropriate in some situations, such as evacuating a building during a fire or leading a platoon charge up the hill, it makes little sense in many others. When the leader doesn't have all the pertinent information, when follow-through may be an issue, and/or maintaining the group's commitment is important, a John Wayne style is often counter-productive.

• *Voting.* Highly valued as "democratic procedure," voting as a decision-making tool in working groups has serious disadvantages as well as some advantages. After subcommittees have made their reports and the matter is talked over as much as time allows, the usual procedure is for the leader to call for a vote after appropriate motions have been made, if parliamentary procedure is followed. Or perhaps someone becomes frustrated if the discussion drags on too long and "calls the question." A vote is taken, and the majority wins. The problem is that the minority loses. The procedure divides the group and creates winners and losers, with the losers less likely to feel committed to the decision. In fact they may do all they can to sabotage or overturn it. The procedure does have the advantage of bringing discussion to a final end point and clearly defining the next step. However, whenever possible compromise and integrative problem solving should be considered.

• *Compromise.* The concept of compromise is simple: nobody gets everything they want, but everybody gets something. Nobody wins completely; nobody loses out. By dividing the various proposals and trading and reassembling elements in different ways a compromise may be struck that provides a reasonable solution while partially satisfying all parties.

A subset of compromise is negotiation. In some cases, groups come together for the explicit purpose of compromising to resolve pre-existing differences. In these cases a neutral third party and the techniques of conflict resolution may be involved to get a compromise accepted. Win/lose outcomes in these situations may result in strikes or business failures.

• *Integrative problem solving or creative problem solving.* In compromise situations the result often serves to satisfy the differing parties but provides only a barely adequate solution. Integrative or creative problem solving allows for the possibility of a solution better than those originally proposed. It relies on synergy, creativity, and group skills to see new possibilities, put things together in new ways, and invent new approaches without the disadvantages of the old ones. It is not possible to write a formula for creative group problem solving. But some of the key elements are members who are highly motivated to find a better way, high levels of substantive expertise, and a group climate that supports openness and risk taking.

Feasibility Testing

Once a decision is made, the group, in weariness and relief, may adjourn with the happy assumption that someone else will follow through. The group's work, however, is not completed. After a brief recess (to clear heads) it is often useful to return for an objective review of the feasibility of the decision. A good approach is to mentally walk it through the stages of implementation. Will it really work? Did we get carried away? (Remember the risky shift phenomenon?) Did we overlook any pitfalls? Have we accounted for all of the variables? Do we need to reopen the discussion to iron out problems? Only after passing this test should the group progress to the next stage.

Plans for Follow-Through

The best decision ever made is worthless unless it is implemented. And implementation cannot be counted on to happen automatically. What is the next step? Who is responsible? When will it be done? How will we know if it is working? It is important for the group to see that follow-through mechanisms are in place. Even if next steps are specifically delegated to others, it is useful to stipulate that the group wants a progress report by a specified time.

Reviewing the Process

Don't adjourn yet! There's one final step. This will probably not be the last decision the group will deal with. Certainly individual members will be involved in many more decision-making situations. What did we learn from this experience? If we had it to do over again, what would we do differently? How committed do we feel to the decision we made? Effective group decision making develops as the group practices and *critiques its experiences.* The discipline of spending a few minutes reviewing the process will pay off.

SUMMARY

In this chapter we have looked at the conditions and techniques that help groups make timely and informed decisions in order to solve problems. We noted that the material in earlier chapters about group dynamics, processes, and leadership is highly relevant to problem solving. Disorganized, unmotivated, poorly led groups are unlikely to make good decisions.

The traditional rational decision-making procedures work well in some situations, but often are not much help with the typical problems that characterize the real world we live in. A series of considerations, or stages, were outlined which provide a rough road map to follow. These 13 steps do not, of course, guarantee that the right decision will be made. But if they are understood and if all members of the group commit themselves to them, they will greatly increase the probability that effectiveness will develop.[8]

LEARNING AIDS

1. Think of a problem one of your groups has dealt with recently. Review the group's problem-solving behavior by evaluating its performance on each of the 13 steps:
    1. Building a climate that supports problem solving
    2. Problem finding
    3. Clarification
    4. Testing members' reactions
    5. Identification of necessary resources
    6. Categorizing the problem
    7. Sharing information and feelings
    8. Looking out for pitfalls in the process
    9. Moving from divergence to convergence
    10. Making the decision
    11. Feasibility testing
    12. Plans for follow-through
    13. Reviewing the process

2. Plan your strategy for working with a group to solve an upcoming problem you have identified. Describe how you will help the group deal with each of the 13 steps.

3. Refer again to the 13 steps. Which of these do you feel most capable of dealing with? Least capable? What steps can you take to improve your skills?

NOTES

1. Renis Likert, *New Patterns of Management* (New York: McGraw-Hill, 1961), p. 166.

2. I do not know the origin of the term "working the problem." I first heard it used in the early 1970s by Sheldon Davis, then vice-president for industrial relations for TRW Systems. Harold Leavitt uses it in the fourth edition of his book, *Managerial Psychology* (Chicago, IL: University of Chicago Press, 1978).

3. Edgar Schein, *Organizational Psychology*, 3d ed. (Englewood Cliffs, NJ: Prentice-Hall, 1980).

4. Harold Leavitt, *Managerial Psychology*.

5. B. R. Patton and K. Griffin, *Decision-Making Group Interaction* (New York: Harper & Row, 1978), p. 135.

6. The relative advantages of group versus individual decision making have been discussed by Jay Hall in "Decisions, Decisions, Decisions," *Psychology Today* 5 (November, 1971), p. 6. Briefly, groups surpass individuals when pooling information and correcting errors occurs through group interaction.

7. D. A. Kolb, "On Management and the Learning Process," in *Organizational Psychology: A Book of Readings*, 3d ed., D. A. Kolb, I. W. Rubin, and J. M. McIntyre, eds. (Englewood Cliffs, NJ: Prentice-Hall, 1979).

8. For a different but compatible problem-solving model, see Frances L. Uslschak, L. Nathanson, and P. G. Gillan, *Small Group Problem Solving: An Aid to Organizational Effectiveness* (Reading, MA: Addison-Wesley, 1981).

8

SPECIAL APPLICATIONS
OF GROUP TECHNIQUES

The importance of group behavior in contemporary organizations is demonstrated by the many special applications of group technology. In this chapter we will examine some of the popular current uses, with an eye to applying principles developed in earlier chapters. We will be discussing:

- *Conducting meetings.* Planning and running meetings to maximize efficiency and productivity.

- *Team building.* Training techniques to develop team skills, and reduce barriers to collaboration.

- *Temporary systems.* Managing task forces, project teams, and matrix structures.

- *Quality circles.* Utilizing worker committees to reduce errors, improve quality, and solicit suggestions for productivity improvement.

- *Autonomous work groups.* Operating with groups that plan, supervise, and evaluate their own functioning.

- *Structured formats.* Techniques for planning and making decisions.

• *Groups for support and learning.* Groups that help members solve their problems and develop as individuals.

MEETINGS

Managers spend a great deal of time in meetings and are often frustrated with the time expended and lack of results. Studies on time management consistently indicate that meetings rank near the top (along with telephone calls) as a major time waster. Too frequently, goals and ground rules are not clear, there is chit-chat that is unrelated to the topic, some members talk much more than necessary while others say nothing, and time runs out before the issue is resolved. Some managers, in exasperation, try to avoid meetings, but that is futile for most of us. Managers can at least strive to make the meetings they hold as efficient and useful as possible. Many practitioners and writers have proposed ideas for improving the effectiveness of meetings. Some presume there are quick, short-range ways to bring meetings out of the doldrums, like carefully arranging where people sit or appointing someone to summarize. But human behavior being what it is, achieving effective meetings is a building and learning process that takes time.

Here is my laundry list of keys to having successful meetings. It builds on ideas we have discussed earlier in this book and emphasizes the role of leader as a skilled group facilitator.

1. Remember that meetings are group phenomena, and that people come with more than just information about the topic. They bring their values, fears, habits, needs, and all the rest of their humanness. It is important to know if and why they are motivated to participate and what their agendas are, and to be on the lookout for problems arising from the group processes we have discussed.

2. Whenever possible, carefully select those who will be present. Many meetings suffer because too many people are present, the wrong people are present, or those present do not bring with them the necessary expertise. Most authorities place the optimal number for a problem-solving meeting at less than eight. Often people are invited because they might feel left out, or their support is needed, or they might hear something useful, or they came last time. There are trade-

offs, of course. If commitment and follow-through are important issues, involvement of a number of individuals may be necessary. However, it is not realistic to expect a meeting of 10 to 20 to solve problems efficiently. It may be necessary to operate in subgroups in order to balance efficiency, commitment, and expertise.

3. Be clear about the purpose of the meeting. Before the meeting, at the beginning, and throughout, if necessary, help the group be clear about why they are meeting, what the problem is, what is expected, what outcome is sought. In many cases, simply writing down the purpose is not adequate. Time may be needed for restatement, clarification, questions. Be sensitive to whether the purpose makes sense to people, and whether they accept it.

4. Be specific about the kind(s) of meeting being held. There are various types of meetings, each with implications for how it is conducted and how time is used.

* *Informational.* Passing along information that participants can use. Often only clarifying or informational questions are to be asked. Such meetings can operate with larger groups and often with less time.

* *Consultation.* Members are asked to discuss, provide their suggestions, identify problems. Someone else will then take action.

* *Problem solving.* The group, through interaction and sharing of information, seeks solutions to problems or charts courses of action.

* *Legislative.* The group, often large, acts to evaluate, approve and perhaps implement proposals brought by subunits.

* *Social–emotional.* The goal is not a product, but to provide support, entertainment, and learning to members.

Several of these may occur in the same meeting, and the leader may segment the agenda so that one portion is informational, another is problem solving, and so on. In any case, it is helpful for members to know what phase they are in and what behavior is appropriate.

5. Build an agenda. An agenda sent out before the meeting is help-ful. A tentative agenda and a request for additional items is even more helpful. Most helpful of all, in my opinion, is a list of tentative agenda items with a few minutes at the beginning of the meeting for building the final agenda on a chalkboard or flip chart, and then pri-oritizing items. Members are more likely to understand and accept the agenda, be sensitive to priorities and time constraints, and feel a sense of responsibility if they are involved in developing the agenda.

6. Clarify the ground rules. These include time availability, level of participation desired, and parliamentary procedure, if any. Will the leader make the decision or will members? Members need to understand what is expected of them and what constraints they are operating under.

7. Keep in mind the stages in group development. We discussed earlier in the book some stages groups are likely to go through as they evolve. Several of these (purpose, control, expectations) have been covered in the points immediately above. In addition, pay atten-tion to identity needs; help people identify themselves and each other so that they will know how they fit in. Encourage a climate of rap-port and support.

8. Help the group transition from divergence to convergence. If the meeting is other than informational, the first part of the session or of any segment may usefully operate at the divergent level for a while; sharing information, generating ideas, suggesting alternatives. At the point when the ideas are all on the table and/or time limits dictate closure, the leader needs to switch the group into a convergent mode. The time has come to pull things together, arrive at a decision, commit to a course of action.

9. Deal with problem members. The bane of most chairpersons is the member whose behavior falls outside the norm—the incessant talker, the dominator, the attacker, the person who can't stay on the subject, the show-off. The bind is that most members recognize and dislike these behaviors, but are reluctant to confront them. They look to the leader to solve the problem, and may lose faith if the leader fails to act. There are, admittedly, value questions involved in coping with "deviant" members. Setting up narrow boundaries for

"acceptable" behavior and punishing those who fail to conform are hardly desirable. On the other hand, those who interfere with others' participation and block group progress cannot be ignored.

Unfortunately there are no sure formulas for dealing with the problem member. In longer-term groups peer pressure may curtail disruptive members. In shorter sessions the chairperson needs to take the lead. There are differing opinions about what to do. My suggestion is a several-stage strategy. The first stage is to do nothing. Often the disruptive member is feeling insecure or wants to establish an identity as a strong member and will recede after an initial outburst. Next, try inattention. Avoid eye contact and do not react to the performance in any manner that reinforces it. Some will receive this subtle message. Next, deal with the behavior: "That was a useful point, now I'd like to hear from some others. I'm sure there are many other good ideas here."

If that fails the next stage is to respond to the person diplomatically, attempting to avoid creating defensiveness. "You've obviously thought a lot about the subject and have strong opioions. Thanks for sharing them with us. I think it's important to move on now to get others' inputs." The final diplomatic stage is to invoke the greater good of the group: "I realize you have strong feelings about the subject, and it is important for us to hear them. I think we've listened responsibly. But there are six others here who have given their time to come to the meeting, and the group cannot function unless everyone has an equal chance. I'm going to move on now and ask you to take your turn in listening to the others." If all of these measures fail there is a real question as to whether the disruptive individual is able or willing to function as a group member. The leader must make a decision about whether the group is strong enough to risk a head-on confrontation, or whether adjournment and a private conference are in order. If nothing is done participation is likely to dwindle and the meeting may fail.

10. Coping with conflict. The second most worrisome problem for many leaders is conflict. In meetings, conflict takes the form of disagreements, impasses, arguments, and hurt feelings. Social scientists have a fairly clear message: Don't try to avoid conflict, it will only smolder and crop up again. Face it, work on it, and try to resolve it.

In the real world of meetings things often seem less simple. Some members dislike or fear conflict and flee from it. Others firmly believe the way to progress is to keep everything on an objective, rational level. Still others bring angry feelings into the session and vent them without commitment to resolving anything. The first thing the leader needs to do is examine her own reaction to conflict. Do you tend to avoid it? Do you get easily drawn into it? Do you believe it can be productive if handled properly? Do you feel reasonably comfortable moving into the middle of a conflict?

The best strategy, in my view, is to let small, apparently transitory conflicts go by without dealing with them the first time, but to respond to them if they recur and grow. The leader can help the group acknowledge the conflict, view it as acceptable, and work on it. The leader might say, "We seem to find ourselves in a conflict about the project. It's not surprising, since we brought differing viewpoints into the meeting on purpose. In fact, when the meeting started we even mentioned that some diagreement was likely. I believe that conflict can be useful if handled well. Let's be sure we have a clear understanding of both points of view. Then we'll see if we can find some common ground. . . ."

Frequently members feel relieved and more comfortable when conflicts are brought out into the open, and the blocked energy, when released, can be helpful in finding solutions.

11. The leader's role. Those who would lead meetings must make a fundamental decision about the role they wish to play. Do you want to be the focus of attention, or do you want the attention to focus on the group? Those who want to be the focus of attention assume a heavy burden, because they necessarily assume a major share of responsibility for having the relevant information, knowing what to do with it, and implementing decisions. Those who would focus the responsibility on the group may, without shirking leadership, act as facilitators who help the total group function at its best. A lifelong expert on meetings, the late Leland P. Bradford, asserted, "meetings work when leadership is conceived as service given to group members as they perform their task."[1]

If there is a useful general principle, it is that successful meetings do not just happen when people enter the room. Planning, careful structuring, and skillful facilitation can make a significant difference.[2]

TEAM BUILDING

Team building is a term used for training sessions to build collaboration skills in groups of people who work together. Few would dream of recruiting two dozen professional football players on Saturday morning and sending them onto the field that afternoon. Even if they were highly skilled in their individual specializations, their lack of training in working together as a team would be a serious detriment. Work teams, however, are frequently assembled from individuals with varying backgrounds and assigned complex tasks that require collaboration without any preparation in teamwork. Team building is a technique that combines training with practice on real problems to help members function together more effectively. A couple of examples will help to explain the concept.

The Up-In-The-Air Corporation has just received a government contract to build a component for a rocket. To get the project started a new project team will be assembled, pulling together experts from various branches and divisions. The head of the team realizes that none of his group has experience working with each other and that serious errors could occur because of garbled communication, confused roles, and professional jealousies. He decides to initiate team-building training at the beginning of the project. The group meets in a week-long retreat setting with a consultant. They get better acquainted and develop a clearer understanding of each others' backgrounds and competencies. They discuss and clarify the role each member will play. They decide how they will deal with potential group problems, such as conflicts. The leader clarifies with the group the assignment, including the corporation's expectations. He also discusses his leadership style and the ground rules about group decision making. At the end of the week the team members have improved their ability to collaborate on the project.

Karen Bowman has been director of the accounting division for four years. The division plays an active role in helping to develop and maintain programs in cost and inventory control in a complex organization. Karen is aware that her staff operates as a stable of individual technicians, not as a team. This can have serious consequences, because projects and assignments are often interrelated, and when staff members do not work together many problems in system coordination arise. The company's director of human resources suggests a team-building project and volunteers to conduct it. Each staff person is interviewed to learn their perspective on departmental functioning and to identify problems in coordination. A day-long session is held in which a teamwork exercise is used to help make members aware of possibilities and barriers to cooperation. The group then discusses ways in which it can improve its teamwork. Two hour follow-up sessions are held each month wherein staff members continue to learn about teamwork and critique their team efforts.

These two examples demonstrate the essence of team building. Through a combination of teaching the elements of group effectiveness, exercises in teamwork, and practice on real organizational issues, members learn to work together as a group. Team building is a component of a body of techniques commonly labeled organization development (OD). They seek to improve organizational functioning by focusing on the human interactional processes involved in getting work done.

Dyer points out that the methodology of team building, or "team development," grew out of the historical blending of the theory of participative management and the methodology of group training techniques, such as sensitivity or T-group training. As we indicated in Chapter 1, management studies in the 1930s, 1940s, and 1950s highlighted the importance of work groups in both individual morale and organization effectiveness. Many of the writers propounded a more open, participative approach to management, including an emphasis on democratic decision making. It was natural, then, for trainers to attempt to use the group training techniques they were developing to enhance organizational effectiveness through better team operation.[3]

TEMPORARY SYSTEMS

A characteristic of many modern organizations is that they utilize a variety of working groups whose existence is a temporary situation, rather than a permanent part of the formal structure. These temporary groups are organized to achieve a specific purpose and usually go out of existence when they have completed their work. Members are brought together on either a full-time or part-time basis to comprise a specific blend of expertise, experience, viewpoint, or implementation capability. They are expected to pool their knowledge and skill and attain objectives that no formal unit in the organization could achieve. Such systems are characteristic of the more flexible, innovative style of management being practiced by many organizations. They rely heavily on members' ability to function effectively in group settings.

One variety of temporary system is the task force, usually formed for the purpose of attacking a problem. They most frequently require a part-time commitment by members drawn together because of their ability to contribute to solving a problem. One authority points out that the distinguishing characteristics of task forces in contrast to ordinary committees are that they are formed to accomplish a task; they are temporary; they have operational responsibility to accomplish something, not just make suggestions; and they build collaboration by cutting across departmental boundaries and professional disciplines. This authority, Thomas L. Quick, also indicates they often have higher levels of autonomy than ordinary committees and make decisions by consensus—qualities that are desirable but true only in some situations.[4]

Kunde provides a case study that demonstrates use of task forces in local government.[5] During the late 1960s and early 1970s urban areas began to experience many problems that traditional city governments were not organized to handle. Problems such as racial unrest, declining population, loss of economic base, and deterioration of housing stock were serious issues in Dayton, Ohio, as in many other communities. The existing structure and procedures appeared to be making little headway in resolving these problems. Officials decided a new approach was needed. A "Task Force on Task Forces" was created, and based on critical community issues identified by the elected city council, it created nine task forces: Youth, Racism, Crime, Housing, Economic Development, Downtown Dayton, Future, and Organizational Improvement.

Membership on each task force was balanced by level, age, race, sex, and organizational unit. Chairpersons were assigned on the basis of leadership ability and were not necessarily experts on the subject matter. Task forces developed goals and a work plan and appointed a process facilitator to encourage team effectiveness. Members' compensation was based equally on performance on the regularly assigned job and performance of the task force. A full-time task force coordinator was appointed. Members were trained in communication, decision making, and other teamwork skills, and a consultant worked with the system on an ongoing basis.

The task force effort in Dayton lasted for two years. Many positive outcomes were reported as were some problems. New programs were developed, often in cooperation with community groups, and policy changes were made in the way the city operated. According to Kunde, the involvement of employees at all levels in the most significant issues of the organization also had a positive impact on the internal operations because it opened communication across units, levels, and subgroups.

Another variety of temporary system is the project team. Although similar to, or indistinguishable from, task forces in some situations, the project team is usually assembled to take responsibility for the management of a project from inception to conclusion. Rather than solving a specific problem or coming to grips with an issue, its role is to handle a project—the design and manufacture of a machine, the development of a new system, the creation of an organizational unit. An example of a project team is illustrated in the Up-In-The-Air Corporation vignette a few pages ago.

Project teams often occur within the framework of "matrix structures," organizational designs in which specialists are affiliated with traditional functional units (design, engineering, finance, manufacturing, marketing) but are also assigned to interdisplinary teams to pool their talents on projects. Thus, individuals operate within a matrix of departments and projects, and are deployed as needed to operate in a temporary grouping for a particular purpose.[6]

Many organizations that utilize task forces or project teams have learned that simply bringing together people with appropriate subject matter knowledge does not assure productivity. Employees who operate in these settings must be able to form new groups that begin to function quickly and to develop comfort in operating in ambiguous situations where reporting lines are complex and authority overlapping. They need skills in teamwork. It is a common finding that operations that rely on temporary systems experience difficulty unless training is provided to members. Team building is often used, and includes such components as communication, group problem solving, and planning.

QUALITY CIRCLES

Quality circles (OCs) or *Quality control circles* are a group application of participative management. Although quality circles achieved notoriety during the Japanese management popularity of the early 1980s,[7] they have been in operation in Japan since the 1960s and are actually renamed versions of employee committees, which have been around for many years. Joe Scanlon, a U.S. labor leader, developed a plan for organizational cooperation and participation during the depression of the 1930s.[8] One central feature of the Scanlon Plan was a series of production committees, composed of labor and management representatives, which met regularly to receive suggestions and discuss ways of cutting costs and improving productivity. The participation philosophy underlying the Scanlon Plan was probably ahead of its time. That, plus the fact that the plan was, in part, a profit-sharing system that evoked both labor and management bias, kept the concept from being widely utilized.

The quality circle is a committee of employees who work in the same unit. They meet regularly on company time to discuss work problems and suggest ways of improving efficiency, effectiveness and morale. QC programs are usually instituted at the top of the organization, where the philosophy of open communication and employee participation must be accepted. Kitvo lists the organizational supports necessary for effective operation of quality circles.[9] Organizational policies and climate must allow employees to:

• Obtain the freedom to say what they think without fear of reprisal, either overt or subtle;

• Discuss concerns with colleagues;

• Meet and work with management;

• Seek information about their jobs;

• Influence decisions made about the quality and quantity of their work;

- See the results of their work; and

- Receive appropriate recognition for success.

Experience suggests several other considerations that are important in implementing a QC program. Quality circles are not just elaborate suggestion systems. They accept responsibility for continually monitoring their part of the operation and striving to improve it. They often have at least limited authority to implement improvements, and usually they do not receive cash rewards for achievements. Since membership in a quality circle often represents for first-line employees a new way of thinking about one's work role, thorough orientation and training is important. There may be initial suspicion that the effort is just another public relations program, or that managers will retaliate if their operations are criticized. Employees may have little experience operating in "sit down groups," and require training in meeting procedures and problem solving. And, expectedly, managers may be threatened by the new alternative power systems and require help in working with them rather than against them.

Whether quality circles portend a fundamental change in the way organizations utilize human resources or just a faddish use of committees remains to be seen.[10] The manager who wishes to experiment with them will be well served by remembering that they are groups that are governed by and limited by the principles we have discussed.

AUTONOMOUS WORK GROUPS

Yet another wrinkle in the use of groups is the *autonomous work group*, sometimes called the *semi-autonomous group*. One of the first widely publicized accounts of the technique is Walton's description of a Topeka, Kansas, pet-food factory.[11] In an older plant owned by the corporation, work was organized in traditional fashion: a hierarchical, authoritarian management system, narrowly defined jobs that were unrewarding at most levels of the need hierarchy, little involvement of employees in decision making. Work performance indicated several signs of serious worker alienation: waste, shutdowns, inefficiency, sabotage and violence. When a new plant was to be built in another city, management decided to experiment with new organizing systems that might counter the problems of old methods.

Rather than functioning as independent operators, workers were organized into teams of 7 to 14 members and a team leader. Each team performed a set of interrelated tasks. Assignment of individuals to specific tasks was a team decision arrived at by consensus. The teams had the authority to reassign workers and to revise and redesign tasks. They held meetings in which they dealt with manufacturing and personnel problems within their areas, aided by a management information system feeding data directly to the teams. Responsibilities included selecting new team members and counseling those who did not meet standards. Team functions included tasks often handled by staff units—quality control, maintenance and housekeeping, and industrial engineering.

Since the autonomous work teams designed all the task combinations to be equally challenging, it was possible to have a single job classification for all members. Pay raises were related to the number of tasks a team member had mastered. Team representatives participated in the governance of the plant; top management allowed most of the plantwide rules and policies to evolve, rather than handing them down at the beginning.

Experience with results of autonomous work groups in the Walton case study and in a number of other applications indicates positive results: higher productivity per hour, less waste, and more employee contribution to solving problems. There are also some difficulties with autonomous work teams. Not all employees respond positively to higher levels of responsibility and group interdependence. And not all team leaders are comfortable in changing from a traditional foreman role to a democratically oriented facilitator. Further, autonomous work teams are human groups; some succeed more than others, some evolve norms that cause trouble, some get into conflicts. Training for leaders and members in techniques of effective group operation is a necessary step.

STRUCTURED FORMATS

It should be evident that there are some potential problems with the interactive group decision-making model discussed in this book. In situations in which the goal is to solicit members' suggestions or ideas and select from them those that are to be used, several processes can detract from the results. Dominant members may override the ideas of those who are less dominant but have better ideas. Pressure to reach a conclusion may interfere with careful consideration of all information. The groupthink phenomenon may operate to intimidate those who dissent. Various disruptive behaviors may serve to get the group off the subject and create frustration and waste time. And members with low levels of group problem-solving skills, when operating in an unstructured setting, can fail to achieve useful results. Because of these kinds of difficulties group practitioners have sought to devise more structured group techniques which can be applied in certain kinds of situations. In this section we will briefly discuss some of those techniques.

Two simple structured methods for equalizing participation are brainstorming and the round robin. Brainstorming seeks to remove constraints on the flow of ideas by withholding evaluation and argumentation. A leader might invite members to suggest as many possible topics for the upcoming sales conference as they can think of. The leader writes the suggestions on the board as they are given. There is no discussion or criticism at this first stage, only clarifying questions. It is hoped that the spontaneous outflow of ideas will stimulate creativity and the lack of evaluation will encourage members to contribute without inhibition. After the brainstorming the group reviews, critiques, and selects from the ideas they have generated.

The round robin technique simply involves taking turns. In the sales conference planning meeting mentioned above, the leader might ask the members, in the order they are seated around the table, to take turns suggesting one topic each. They continue to contribute topics until everyone has run out of ideas. The suggestions can then be evaluated in the same order, if they wish.

A highly structured technique has been developed that goes considerably beyond brainstorming and the round robin. This is the *nominal group technique* (NGT). We will provide a brief introduction to NGT in this section, leaving the reader who wishes to utilize it to research further in the cited references.[12]

The nominal group technique may be used with a group of up to 10, or with several such groups in a conference setting. The goal, to continue our theme, may be to select five program topics for an upcoming sales conference that will best assist the sales force in improving their performance. In the first step of the NGT process members are asked to reflect and silently write their program ideas. The second stage is a round robin recording of these ideas on a flip chart.

Step 3 is a serial discussion of each of the ideas recorded, with the goal of clarifying and exploring each one. In step 4 members vote, on paper, and then rank the five items they believe contain the best ideas. These votes are tallied and the items most highly ranked are again discussed in step five. Step 6 is a final vote, in which members choose five items from the remaining list and give them numerical weights. The five with the highest total weighting are the topics that will be covered at the sales conference.

The nominal group technique avoids many of the group decision-making pitfalls we mentioned earlier in this section. A structure is imposed that assures more nearly equal participation. The two written votes minimize domination by a few. The serial discussions provide an opportunity to consider each suggestion in some depth. The leader plays an active role in orchestrating and keeping time and thus can keep the meeting within pre-established time limits.

There are also some disadvantages. The NGT structure narrows the range of behaviors. While it reduces the chances for negative group influences, it may lessen the possibility of creative problem solving, synergy, and productive conflict. It also controls the group's activities rather than dealing with process issues, a possible problem in long-term groups. Nevertheless, many group trainers have found NGT a valuable tool for use in conferences and program-planning situations in which a number of discrete items must be selected from a longer list of possibilities.

There are, of course, other structured group systems. Probably the most common is parliamentary procedure. As I have indicated before, parliamentary procedure is useful in large meetings where the purpose is deliberative and legislative—to receive, discuss, and act on proposals brought forth by subgroups. But it often hampers free discussion and problem solving in smaller working groups. And it may be used by those who wish to stay in control, as in this excerpt from Mike Royko's description of how Mayor Daley dealt with the Chicago city council:

It is his council, and in all the years it has never once defied him as a body. . . .

He looks down at them, bestowing a nod or a benign smile on a few favorites, and they smile back gratefully. . . . When the minority goes on the attack, one of the administration aldermen he has groomed for the purpose will rise and answer the criticism by shouting that the critic is a fool, a hypocrite, ignorant, and misguided. Until his death, one alderman could be expected to leap to his feet at every meeting and cry, "God bless our mayor, the greatest mayor in the world."

But sometimes Keane and his trained orators can't shut down the minority, so Daley has to do it himself. If provoked, he'll break into a rambling, ranting speech, waving his arms, shaking his fists, defending his judgment, defending his administration, always with the familiar "It is easy to criticize . . . to find fault . . . but where are your programs . . . where are your ideas. . . ."

If that doesn't shut off the critics, he will declare them to be out of order, threaten to have the sergeant at arms force them into their seats, and invoke *Robert's Rules of Order*, which, in the heat of debate, he once described as "the greatest book ever written."

All else failing, he will look toward a glass booth above the spectator's balcony and make a gesture known only to the man in the booth who operates the sound system that controls the microphones on each alderman's desk. The man in the booth will touch a switch and the offending critic's microphone will go dead and stay dead until he sinks into his chair and closes his mouth.[13]

GROUPS FOR SUPPORT AND LEARNING

It doesn't seem right to complete this book without at least a mention of the many current uses of groups to help their members learn, change, cope, or heal. Even though these groups may not be working groups in a technical sense, they are relevant to work in a number of ways. The list is extensive: sensitivity training groups (T-groups, encounter groups); therapy groups; Alcoholics Anonymous groups; support groups for divorce, grief, and other dilemmas; groups for married people, single people, old people, young people; drug rehabilitation groups; prison groups; and groups for people who run groups.[14]

We know that groups are capable of wielding powerful influence over members, for better or worse. It has been my privilege to work with many managers in T-group programs of the National Training Laboratories, and to see them achieve higher levels of self-understanding and sensitivity to others through process-oriented techniques developed by the pioneers of group training.[15] Many of us have seen friends or colleagues brought back from the despair of alcoholism or drug abuse through the compassion and strength of rehabilitation groups. Still others of us know people who were lifted from depression and hopelessness by groups with a therapeutic purpose. Unfortunately, some of us have also seen young people led away from their families and communities by fanatical religious groups, and military prisoners brainwashed, in part through the use of groups.

It is likely that sometime in the future you or someone close to you will seek out a group for assistance in dealing with life's problems. Insist on groups led by qualified professionals—licensed mental health personnel or individuals sanctioned by respected institutions such as hospitals, colleges, or established churches. Beware of claims of quick and dramatic cures. Human change takes work, patience, and courage.

It is almost certain that you will spend a good deal of your work life in groups. I hope that this book will help you function in them more effectively. More than that, I hope your increased understanding will help you enjoy groups more.

NOTES

1. Leland P. Bradford, *Making Meetings Work: A Guide for Leaders and Group Members* (San Diego, CA: University Associates, 1976).

2. For additional reading on meetings see Anthony Jay, "How to Run a Meeting," *Harvard Business Review* (March–April, Vol. 54, 1976): 43–57; Richard J. Dunsing, *You and I Have Simply Got to Stop Meeting this Way* (New York: American Management Association, 1978); Eva Schindler-Rainman, Ronald Lippitt, and Jack Cole, *Taking Your Meetings Out of the Doldrums* (San Diego, CA: University Associates, 1975).

3. William G. Dyer, *Team Building: Issues and Alternatives* (Reading, MA: Addison-Wesley, 1977). See also W. L. French and C. H. Bell, Jr., *Organization Development: Behavioral Science Interventions for Organization Improvement*, 2d ed. (Englewood Cliffs, NJ: Prentice-Hall, 1978).

4. Thomas L. Quick, *Your Role in Task Force Management: The Dynamics of Corporate Change* (Garden City, NY: Doubleday, 1972).

5. James Kunde, "Task Force Management in Dayton, Ohio," in *Organization Development in Public Administration: Part II, Public Sector Applications of Organization Development Technology*, R. T. Golembiewski and W. B. Eddy, eds. (New York: Marcel Dekker, 1978), pp. 218–26.

6. For a fuller discussion of nontraditional work systems see Chris Argyris, "Today's Problems with Tomorrow's Organizations," *Journal of Management Studies* 4 (1967): 31–55. Reprinted in W. B. Eddy and W. W. Burke, eds., *Behavioral Science and the Manager's Role*, 2d ed. (San Diego, CA: University Associates, 1980).

7. W. G. Ouchi, *Theory Z.* (New York: Avon Books, 1981).

8. Carl F. Frost, J. H. Wakeley, and R. A. Ruh, *The Scanlon Plan for Organization Development; Identity, Participation and Equity* (East Lansing, MI: Michigan State University Press, 1974).

9. Roger Ritvo, "Managing with Quality Circles," in *The NTL Managers Handbook*, R. A. Ritvo and Alice G. Sargent, eds. (Arlington, VA: NTL Institute for Applied Behavioral Science, 1983).

10. Ralph Barra, *Putting Quality Circles to Work* (New York: McGraw-Hill, 1983); Laurie Fitzgerald and J. Murphy, *Installing Quality Circles: A Strategic Approach* (San Diego, CA: University Associates, 1982).

11. Richard E. Walton, "How to Counter Alienation in the Plant," *Harvard Business Review* 50 (November–December, 1972): 70–81; "Work Innovations at Topeka: After Six Years," *Journal of Applied Behavioral Science* 13 (1977): 422–33.

12. Andre L. Delbecq, A. H. Van de Ven, and D. H. Gustafson, *Group Techniques for Program Planning: A Guide to Nominal Group and Delphi Processes* (Glenview, IL: Scott, Foresman and Co., 1975); A. H. Van de Ven and A. L. Delbecq, "Nominal vs. Interacting Group Processes for Committee Decision-Making," *Academy of Management Journal* 14 (June 1971).

13. Mike Royko, *Boss: Richard Daley of Chicago* (New York: New American Library, Signet, 1971), 19–20.

14. For an analysis of the origin and function of various helping groups see W. B. Eddy and B. Lubin, "Laboratory Training and Encounter Groups," *Personnel and Guidance Journal* 49 (1971): 625–35.

15. Leland P. Bradford, J. R. Gibb, and K. D. Benne, eds., *T-Group Theory and Laboratory Method: Innovation in Re-Education* (New York: Wiley, 1964).

INDEX

participation, 6
perception, 24–25
  selective perception, 32
  self-perception, 34
power, 45–46, 87–88
  expert power, 3
  legitimate power, 88
  position power, 88, 97
  reward and punishment
    power, 88
prejudice, 46–47
pressure, social, 33
primary group, 4
problem finding, 143
problem members, 160–61
problem solving, 139
  convergence and diver-
    gence, 149–50
  integrative problem
    solving, 152
  stages in problem solving,
    142
problem working, 142
process of group interaction,
  63, 111
psychological contract, 75

Q

quality circles, 9, 167
Quick, T. L., 165

R

rationality, 20, 42

reality, perception of, 21
risk, 72
risky shift phenomenon, 123
Roethlisberger, Fritz, 5
roles of group members, 76–77
  individual roles, 79–80
  maintenance roles, 78
  task roles, 78

S

Schein, E., 75
Schon, D., 36
Schutz, W., 71
self-concept, 22–23
self-esteem, 22–23
self-oriented behavior, 30–31,
  79–80
sensitivity training, 6
sexuality, 49, 130–31
small group, 2
social-emotional issues, 61,
  111–12
social system, 58–59
stereotype, 32
structure, 8–9, 44, 97
synergy, 18

T

T-group, 172
Tannenbaum, R., & S. Davis,
  52
task force, 3, 165

team: management team, 3
    project team, 3
team building, 163–64
temporary systems, 164–66
Theory X and Y, 90–91
Trist, E., 7
trust, 24, 65, 73, 128

V

values, 51, 106
Vroom, V. H., 98

W

Western Electric
    Hawthorne Studies, 5
women's role, 48
work group, 3

Y

Yankelovitch, D., 53

ABOUT THE AUTHOR

WILLIAM B. EDDY is Helen Kemper Professor of Administration at the University of Missouri–Kansas City. He has been Associate Dean and Director of Management Development in the School of Business and Public Administration at the University of Missouri–Kansas City and Associate Director of the Federal Executive Institute in Charlottesville, Virginia.

Dr. Eddy has published widely in the area of behavioral science applied to management. He is author or editor of several books, including *Public Organizational Behavioral and Development* (Little, Brown) and *Handbook of Organization Management* (Marcel Dekker), and a number of articles, and has been coeditor of the journal *Administration and Society*. He also consults and conducts management training for corporations and agencies.

Dr. Eddy holds B.S. and M.S. degrees from Kansas State University and a Ph.D. in Industrial Psychology from Michigan State University. He is a Fellow of the American Psychological Association and a licensed organizational psychologist.